PN Review 233

VOLUME 43   NUMBER 3   JANUARY–

--------------------------------- R E P O R T S ---------------------------------

--------------------------------- P O E M S   &   F E A T U R E S ---------------------------------

--------------------------------- J O H N   F U L L E R   A T   8 0 :   A   C E L E B R A T I O N ---------------------------------

--------------------------------- R E V I E W S ---------------------------------

C O V E R ---------------------------------

MASKULL LASSERRE, *Improbable Worlds* (2015). A piano is cut almost in half, leaving a wishbone-shaped bridge at its centre. 'The remaining wood that tenuously joins the two halves of the instrument carries a burden of anxiety, potential and hope,' writes Lasserre. Photograph courtesy of the artist.

Editorial

With this issue *PN Review* announces the appointment of its first artist in (virtual) residence, the American composer Michael Hersch.

This eccentric development is the result of a reading and concert celebrating the life and work of Christopher Middleton at St Saviour's Church, St George's Square, London, on 28 May 2016. Michael's *a tower in air* for soprano and horn (with Ah Young Hong and Michael Atkinson), containing lines from Middleton's poetry, was premiered, along with sections from his sonata *The Vanishing Pavilions*, also grounded in the poetry.

Described by Andrew Clark in the *Financial Times* as 'one of the most fertile musical minds to emerge in the U.S. over the past generation', Michael will work with *PN Review* to create a musical commission including poetry. The beginning of his residency is marked by Marius Kociejowski's feature in these pages, and will chart Michael's course over the coming years, with wider attention to connections between contemporary music and poetry. This 'natural musical genius who continues to surpass himself' (Tim Page, *Washington Post*) will visit Europe during his residency, and events will be organised around him.

Born in Washington D.C. in 1971, Michael came to international attention aged twenty-five when he received the Concordia American Composers Award. He is one of the youngest ever recipients of a Guggenheim Fellowship in Composition. He was also awarded the Prix de Rome, the Berlin Prize and the Goddard Lieberson Fellowship from the American Academy of Arts and Letters. His work has been performed around the world under distinguished conductors including Mariss Jansons, Alan Gilbert and Marin Alsop. He has written for soloists including Patricia Kopatchinskaja, Thomas Hampson and Midori. His solo and chamber works are performed around the globe – from the Lincoln Center and Carnegie Hall in the United States to Germany's Schloss Neuhardenberg Festival in Brandenburg and the Philharmonie in Berlin; from Dartington New Music Festival to Italy's Romaeuropa and Nuova Consonanza Festivals and Japan's Pacific Music Festival. Michael is a most welcome presence in *PNR*.

*

We also mark in this issue, with a supplement, the eightieth birthday of the poet John Fuller. In an age in which Creative Writing programmes sometimes seem to bankroll foundering English departments, how is it that Oxford, without (until lately) a formal Creative Writing offering, has produced so many outstanding contemporary poets (and novelists), a disproportionate number having come through Magdalen College? One answer is to be found in Magdalen's long-lived Florio Society, now open to the wider university, and its quondam English Fellow John Fuller, an Augustan spirit, who continues to attend the Society.

Even half a century ago, when I was an undergraduate at a different college, John Fuller was at work.

His little hand press, the Sycamore Press, located in John's garage, was starting to turn out booklets and broadsheets that have marked a dozen important debuts. The debutants typeset, guillotined, folded and sewed their own and one another's verses. John was editing Auden and writing poems, a quiet and significant figure who continues animating a new – a fourth – generation of writers, ensuring that their engagement with English poetry in all its kinds and periods is a mainspring of their creative enterprise. His wry, critically encouraging example flows so contrary to the dominant currents of the age, and so effective has been his creative challenge, as teacher, editor, poet and poetic collaborator (collaboration is one of his chief creative and pedagogic activities, the pedagogy running in both directions), that it is hard to imagine how British poetry could have coped without him.

Here's to his next eighty years!

*

'She was intensely private and though she died – apparently a few days ago in Illinois – of recurrent illness, there was no chatter at all about it,' Eavan Boland wrote to me of the death in October of Brigit Pegeen Kelly (1951–2016). It was Eavan who recommended her work to this magazine, where we featured in 2007 and 2008 a dozen of her major poems, and Carcanet published her two American collections in a single volume, *Poems: Song and The Orchard*, in 2008. We were surprised that her death passed with so little notice. In my view, she is a figure whose small *oeuvre* belongs on the shelf reserved for the work of Marianne Moore and Elizabeth Bishop, two equally careful, equally troubled writers.

'I admired her so much,' Eavan wrote. 'Occasionally I wished she were more in the world of publication/presence/exposure. I feared she wouldn't publish more and would become – and in a way she did – the hermetic figure which was always in her heart. [...] When I think of her work I like to think of "Three Cows and the Moon" best – the poem at the end of *Song*. It has an expansive, pastoral ease in the world that isn't always in the more gothic poems. And it breathes with a sort of happiness I always felt she didn't have enough of. [...] She was a poet's poet's poet and I will miss her greatly.'

As Eavan suggests, there is a sort of justice in the media's neglect of Kelly's passing. She's in a class of her own, which is where she wanted to be, as little as possible trammeled by contemporary nostrums. Her prosody is inventive and brilliant, her diction scrupulously woven, of a piece. Her sense of a human condition in which evil is a real, contending force, colours the work: deeply Christian but with a Redeemer so retiring that He often counts as an absence. In her world a mother raises her children, creatures suffer, and the beauties of creation are exquisite and sometimes unbearable. The poems remind us how serious poetry can be, even if it is smiling, how much it can demand of the writer and give the attentive reader.

News & Notes

Richard Howard · has received the *Paris Review*'s Lifetime Achievement Award for his contribution to literature. His sixteen collections of poetry include *Untitled Subjects*, which received the 1970 Pulitzer Prize. His translations introduced Roland Barthes, Michel Foucault, and E. M. Cioran to Anglophone readers. His Baudelaire *Les fleurs du mal* won a National Book Award in 1983; and more recently the later novels of Guy de Maupassant have occupied him. It is appropriate that the *Paris Review* recognise in this fashion their one-time poetry editor (1992–2005) and Chevalier de l'Ordre National du Mérite.

Ida Vitale · the Uruguayan writer, now ninety-two years old, received the 2016 Federico García Lorca International Prize of the City of Granada, and suggested to the judges that part of the prize was for her industrious persistence. 'Spain has been very generous to me, but this feels like almost too much,' she said, having last year won the Queen Sofia Prize, and the year before the Alfonso Reyes Prize in Mexico. Born in Montevideo (birthplace of Laforgue, Supervielle and many other poets) in 1923, she has been at the heart of Uruguayan and Latin American poetry for several generations.

She admitted that she found the award of this year's Nobel Prize for literature to Bob Dylan 'strange'. 'If they were considering specifically that conjunction of words and music, there would be many Latin American candidates.' She suggested the Chilean Violeta Parra. But she does not endorse the conjunction of words and music in the context of a major literary award. Of course the two arts go hand in hand and sometimes combine – what better example than Lorca himself – but she adds, 'Poetry is not so successfully protected a species as to leave it exposed. Poetry prizes are for poets, not song-writers, just as awards for architecture are not given to painters. Breaking with tradition is fine, but it's not always the best way forward.' Yo Zushi writing in the *New Statesman* (14 October) was less charitable to the judges, more mordant. He follows Dylan's prize history from 1963 when he gracelessly accepted the Tom Paine Award from the National Emergency Civil Liberty's Committee, expressing sympathy for Lee Harvey Oswald (John Kennedy had been assassinated in the same year). He has accumulated prizes, 'Grammies, the Polar Music Prize, an Oscar, the MusiCares Person of the Year Award, among others. Dylan likes awards. Unlike Sartre, he doesn't worry about becoming an institution, or how it might inhibit his creativity. After his endlessly beguiling minor-key stomper "Things Have Changed" won the Academy Award for Best Original Song in 2001, he started displaying the gold statuette onstage at gigs, seemingly glued on top of an amp.' Yo Zushi quotes Irvine Welsh, who condemned the Nobel Committee's decision 'as one that was "wrenched from the rancid prostates of senile, gibbering hippies"'. But Yo Zushi is not quite so unkind. He is in fact a fan, and he disapproves of the award *as* a fan. 'As he once said himself, he is above all else a "song

and dance man". He dabbled in poetry and bashed out a sort of novel in the late sixties called *Tarantula*, which was fun but only gestured towards what he could do onstage or in a recording studio. That wasn't enough for him and, even as a fan, those experiments aren't enough for me. I suspect that many of those who fixate on his words scour his songs as texts, looking for poetry in conventional terms at the expense of the performance. (I won't name names, but you know who you are.) I wonder whether they hear the music at all, and the voice at the centre of it. The irony is that what poetry exists on Dylan's records is largely to be found in the sound of the words, not their meaning. Music – no, Dylan's version of music – alchemises those lyrics into great art. He's a great singer. His genius is in that sand and glue.'

Rodolfo Hinostroza · The celebrated Peruvian cook, astrologer and poet of the radical 1960s generation Rodolfo Hinostroza (1941–2016) has died in Lima. He set out to study medicine but poetry sidetracked him and he changed course and courses at university, receiving a scholarship to study English literature in Cuba (before the Revolution). He became a significant innovator in Peruvian writing, spending some years in France as a translator and broadcaster. He wrote a novel, also, and was an essayist, story-writer and dramatist.

Lucia Perillo · a poet who lived with multiple sclerosis since 1988 and was much concerned with death, died on 16 October at the age of fifty-eight. Her publisher, the increasingly legendary Copper Canyon Press, announced the news. Earlier in 2016 her collection *Time Will Clean the Carcass Bones* was highly praised by reviewers. Her 'shrewd, well-organized free verse', the *New York Times* said, 'marches straight down the page while its meanings peel off in multiple directions'. In 2000, as a MacArthur Foundation fellowship recipient, she was praised by the poet Rodney Jones in the *Chicago Tribune*: 'Her goal is lucidity. She does not like the idea of writing a poem that people cannot understand.'

David Antin · On 11 October the poet and performance artist David Antin, known for his 'talk poems', extemporized narratives and reflections, and celebrated by some critics, in particular Marjorie Perloff, died in La Jolla, California. He was eighty-four. It was in the 1970s that Antin began to evolve his characteristic form combining a kind of poetry, narrative and reflective essay, recording these performed pieces, transcribing and editing them. His first collection in this mode, called simply *Talking* (1972), was followed by *Talking at the Boundaries* (1976), *Tuning* (1984) and *What It Means to Be Avant-Garde* (1993). A vivid conversationalist, he remained a controversial figure due to the form of composition he practsced and the formatting of his work when it settled on the page. At sixteen he was drawn to the work of Gertrude Stein, and his practice might be seen as living out a direction suggested by her later work. He studied as a linguist and worked as a translator from German and Russian. He was a founder of the *Chelsea Review* where he was exposed to the work of Laura Riding Jackson. He wrote about the arts, early on considering Andy Warhol, Sol LeWitt and Roy Lichtenstein among others, and his best essays are collected in *Radical Coherency* (2011). He taught in the visual arts department of the University of California at San Diego for three decades.

Mexico · On 17 October at the marbled Palace of Fine Arts in Mexico City, before its celebrated enormous Tiffany-glass 'curtain' portraying the volcanoes Popocatepetl and Iztaccihuatl, the inaugural world conference of poetry by 'indigenous peoples', 'Voces de Colores para la Madre Tierra', was declared open. It lasted for a week, with readings and encounters at spectacular and historic venues all around the city. The pre-eminent translator of indigenous Mexican (especially Nahuatl) poetry, the nonagenarian anthropologist, historian and linguist Miguel León-Portilla, welcomed delegates drawn from communities in Colombia, Norway, Argentina, Sweden, Finland, Peru, Guatemala, Venezuela, New Zealand, and Mexico itself. The delegates were for the most part poets who compose in the original languages of those countries, as well as sundry ambassadors and members of the Mexican literary community.

The initiative began in 2014 at the celebrated Medellín International Poetry Festival, in Colombia. Mexican writers took up the challenge in what may become an annual gathering. A future conference might add Welsh, Scots Gaelic and Irish (and perhaps Cornish and Manx if poets and funding can be found), as well as African and Asian languages, to the rich Babel of tongues including Náhuatl, Mazateco and Ñuu Savi from Mexico; Quechua from Peru; Sami from Norway, Finland and Sweden; Mapuche from Argentina; Wayuu and Camëntsá from Colombia; and Maorí from New Zealand.

Letters

PETER SCUPHAM WRITES: I was interested to read Thomas Kinsella's revisionist comments on Wordsworth's marriage in his commentary on 'Nutting' (*PNR* 232).

The 'frugal Dame', now identified by Kinsella as the 'attentive, sensible wife' of the poet, reveals at last that Ann Tyson, beloved by William as his Hawkshead landlady, though already married to Hugh Tyson, must have entered into a bigamous relationship with William as a schoolboy, this act in a curious way being a premonition of the poet's extraordinary behaviour in placing the ring with which he was about to marry Mary Hutchinson on his sister Dorothy's finger for a pre-wedding 'wedding' night.

There are wheels within wheels, and I am glad to have watched them spinning so surprisingly, yet agreeably.

THOMAS KINSELLA RESPONDS: Mine is not a commentary on Wordsworth's 'Nutting'. It is a direct response to the poem, on the poem's own terms – with nothing added from Wordsworth's biography.

The central figure is not identifiable in the poem as Wordsworth himself; and in my reading needs to be mature. The sexual psychic experience which is the core of the poem – sensual languor; sudden violence; imagery of virginity and rape; satiation, with awareness of pain – would seem extreme for a young schoolboy.

CHRIS MILLER WRITES: I failed to return a carefully drawn-up list of corrections to the proofs of my essay *i.m.* Yves Bonnefoy (*PNR* 232). Among these corrections was one affecting the last line of the essay, quoting the first poem in Bonnefoy's Douve, '... *ô plus belle/Que la foudre, quand elle tache les vitres blanches de ton sang.*' Here the *de* can be read as 'of' but the reading 'with', as Anthony Rudolf has kindly pointed out, was confirmed by Bonnefoy himself. I am reluctant to allow my error, shared with Galway Kinnell, to stand. Anthony's fine translation is as follows:

And I have seen you break apart and take your pleasure in
    being dead – O you who are more beautiful
Than the lightning, when it stains the white window panes
    with your blood.

ANTHONY RUDOLF WRITES: While not agreeing with every interpretation, I would like to say that Chris Miller's homage to Yves Bonnefoy is a marvellous and singular account of his relationship with this great poet and, equally, with the poet's work.

KATHRYN MARIS WRITES: I disagree with David Spittle's assessment of Jamie McKendrick's work in his *Selected Poems* as 'artfully conjured but stunted' – though I accept that is a matter of opinion. I also disagree with his categorisation of a sonnet as a 'box' as though it's an airless trap or coffin – but that, too, is an opinion. What is less a matter of opinion, however, is the sonnet form itself. Of 'Skin Deep', which Spittle uses to support his judgment of McKendrick's poems, Spittle asks, 'Why a sonnet? Could it not inch its tentacular vision from out of that particular box?' McKendrick's unrhymed, eleven-lined poem doesn't strike me as anything like a 'box', but it is surely not a sonnet.

Poetry Does Not Apply Here

Vahni Capildeo

DURING THE PREPARATIONS for a civil marriage in Oxfordshire in 1999, the couple was encouraged to select readings and music and to write their own ceremony, including the wording of the vows. The nicely suited registrar told them that religious material would, however, be banned. Forget Gerard Manley Hopkins; gag George Herbert. 'What if we don't believe in it?' It might have been the secular Jewish half of the couple who asked. He argued for the intrinsic poetic value of texts and songs. The other half, who had a degree in English language and literature, was upset for other reasons. She argued that systems of wealth and patronage meant that a lot of poetry and music was produced for churches as performance spaces and the congregation as audience. There was nothing to say that the writers and composers were especially religious, rather than writing with or within what had been available and allowed them to earn a living and concentrate on their art. The registrar's rule, strictly applied, therefore would write off centuries, geographies, and communities of artistic production.

No deal. The registrar had no time for the notion of poetry as poetry, or poets as employees. Might lots of gods cancel one other out, thus pacifying the official? If a deity acting alone cannot sneak past the legal radar, how about neutralised divinities? 'What if we have material from several different religions? So it's not as if we're believing in one'. The Wielder of the Pen was absolute: don't mention a G–d. It would be interesting if those who organise National Poetry Day or lobby for school curriculum reform actually spoke to people like this official, whose everyday work intersects with the living and practical use or exclusion of verse. Why and how do ideas of 'poetry' add up, or not, for them?

Forbidden to aestheticise or historicise, the mixed-sceptic couple, to their surprise, felt a cold, vacuum-like whoosh. They realised that although their own beliefs did not match, or did not exist, they wanted a Something. So, they cheated. A friend who was a classical scholar prepared a recitation of Homeric hymns. The registrar scowled, feeling that she had been tricked somehow. Dead languages carry a suspicious aura of holiness. Even more so if they are recited in audible patterns that may not be intelligible but sound beautiful. Shown a translation, she was unable to admit to taking Zeus seriously, though she was culturally sensitive enough to modern times to have banned Lord Vishnu. By invoking the ancient Greek pantheon, the couple may well have committed an act of cultural appropriation, but there were no dead Hellenes to answer back.

1881 and the Canboulay riots in Trinidad and Tobago are more than an act of resistance against the prohibition of street celebrations. They assert African history, presence and continuous creative intervention in the public and private life of the nation.[1] 1883 and British colonial rule bans drumming altogether in Trinidad and Tobago. Drumming is essential to the practice of the polytheistic Orisha religion.

1917 and an Ordinance is passed to 'render illegal indulgence in the practices of the body known as the Shouters'. The syncretistic Spiritual Baptist faith, with its participatory, physical and environmental nature – shaking, shouting, immersion in bodies of water – was legalised only as recently as 1951. It is as if the twin island-colony were a gigantic marriage registry, in which selected gods and associated creative expression, understood to be dangerous, were banned, so that Civility might be espoused.

Huh. Hah. Ah. Kamau Brathwaite, composing his poem 'Xango', may pronounce 'your thunder has come home' (*Black + Blues* (1995; 1976)). In popular culture, too, and on social media, Caribbean arts scene commentators like Geoffrey Philp may identify prodigious figures like the runner Usain 'Lightning' Bolt with particular energies, such as Shango, the fiery, virile thunder-and-lightning Orisha.[2] However, the argument that particular versions of religiosity have been assimilated, mainstreamed or sublimed into Western arts, thus becoming freely available, does not translate for the arts in communities whose once-persecuted metaphorical, belief and behavioural systems have survived, and furnished a means of survival, despite being forbidden. They remain to some extent secret. Even or especially in the crucible of a small island, it is possible to grow up adjacent to such traditions, aware of their resonance, and yet to be unable to write of them without cultural appropriation. So what if one crosses into that realm of expression and experience? Write about it, or not?

Here comes another ox to sit on one's tongue and enforce silence. When well-behaved poets perform, they tend to entertain or move, but not to upset, their listeners – or sponsors. Yes, they can be 'challenging' or 'dark', but in such a way that you come up to them and wring their hands or ask for a signature, not so that you turn away or run. The flip side to the hopeful or admiring question 'Why don't you write about that?' is '...but don't write about *that*'. So what if the subject occupying the writer's mind is both potentially culturally appropriative, and excessive?

August 1, 2016: Emancipation Day. On this day in 1834, the slaves were 'freed' into a four-year apprenticeship of unpaid labour to their former masters. Silence the first, the digital clock marking 3:30 in the morning; hours before the next half-bracket of a bird call. Silence the second, the nonsense talked by the taxi driver; fearing street crime, she loses her way in a grid, and rolls down the window to jitter questions at the wrong types. Silence the third, the pan yard without its steelpans; the site where the ceremony for the ancestors will be held, before the procession with flaming torches, and the historical theatre outdoors. All are welcome; few have heard of it. Silence the fourth, the people, the drummers not yet drumming, whom I do not describe, at the gateway, which you enter; the people, the priests, in the courtyard, whom I also do not describe. Silence the fifth, how minimal each invocation – not noise, but precision of aim and effect. Silence the sixth, when they say 'It is August the first, 1838', and fans start whirring in the brain. Silence the seventh, the numerous people now in the yard, including both sets of dead grandparents, and the out-of-view hill with the indigenous woman starting to lean up on her gigantic, broken elbow. Silence the eighth, when you know you are dying. Silence the ninth, when you remember having been at the ceremony, and wake up to find that we are still there.

Silence the tenth, in which you cross a stone bridge into wilderness to greet the priest who meets you as you wake up where I have been lain down across two chairs. Thou shalt not speak of this to strangers, nor understand what has passed.

---

1 http://caribbean-beat.com/issue-108/rituals-resistance
2 http://geoffreyphilp.blogspot.co.uk/2012/07/usain-bolt-aka-shango.html

---

Letter from Chios

Jamie Osborn

SOUDA CAMP LIES in a moat beneath what is known as 'the castle', Chios's old town. On the other side of the moat is a bank of quiet residential properties and rooms-to-let. The camp's location might be described as sadly 'appropriate', symbolic: welcome to a Europe where refugees are squeezed between defensive walls and backstreets catering for holidaymakers. But here only a kind of vulgarity, bordering violence, is 'appropriate'.

Imad is a former professor of French at a Syrian university who has been in Souda for over six months. Walking towards the fig tree which is his favourite place to sit and read – currently, David Foenkinos's *Charlotte*, the story of a pre-war Jewish family in Berlin – he gestures towards the beach beyond the camp: 'If it were nine hundred dogs living on this beach, all the world's media would be here, believe me,' he says. Then he adds, with the assurance of disillusionment's logic, 'We are human, so Europe treats us worse than dogs'. Meanwhile, politicians make their rounds at distant summits, reiterating calls to distinguish 'economic migrants' from 'genuine refugees'. Such distinctions are projected as both the beginning and end point of a cycle of interrogations to which refugees are subjected in the process of determining their appropriateness to Europe. The cross-examinations that follow call up echoes and shadows that seem intended to confuse. Immediate answers are demanded in interviews, yet the wait for results is allowed to pass into months. On the refugees' part, specific questions of *when* and *how* give way to the repeated, 'Is this Europe?' 'What have we done?' 'Where is the humanity?'

Imad arrived in Chios on 20 March, the date the EU-Turkey deal came into effect and largely prevented onward movement from the Greek islands. Life in the camps is confined to walking in circles while waiting for the date of one's 'eligibility interview' to be announced. Once it is announced, it is changed without the 'PoC' ('Person of Concern') being informed, as happened twice to Imad. Meanwhile, NGO working groups produce circulars reviewing the minutes of their last meeting. 'It is like a snail, my friend', says Methkal, an English literature student, drawing a slow snail's shell in the air. Abu Moufak,

a carpenter, responds by scraping with a blunt knife at the bench he sits on all day, and motions twisting out his heart with the same circling gesture.

When Souda bellies out from the narrow space of the moat to cover the fishing beach with small blue dome tents (the numbers landing in Chios began to rise again a few months after the EU-Turkey deal), the media arrives, as if in defiance of Imad's conviction that only dogs might attract attention. The subsequent BBC News video is titled 'The refugees stuck in Greece's holiday resorts'. Comments on social media point out that 'in no way are these people stuck "in" a holiday resort'. Refugees stroll past the bars and the yachts along the waterfront. They mingle with the day-trippers from Turkey and families from the Gulf, or with local anarchists in 'Billy's' rock bar. On the end of the harbour wall, a crowd of children gathers round an old man with a homemade angling rod. Behind them, young men dive from a tower (a watch-tower or a small lighthouse, it is hard to tell) into the blue water, beautiful bodies against a clear sky.

The water, it is revealed later, is contaminated with sewage allowed to run out of the camp, while among the yachts, the sullen grey military boat used for Frontex patrols is all the more conspicuous for being designed not to glitter. Neo-fascists beat up refugees in the park, with reports of police complicity. The violence feeds on itself: in March, refugees frustrated by their sudden detention under the EU-Turkey deal occupied Chios port for five days, ending in clashes with locals and police. In June, a fire that was started in the Souda camp as a protest against the slowness of the asylum procedures and against living conditions destroyed UNHCR (the UN Refugee Agency) and other NGO tents; in October another fire destroyed the aid organisations' 'containers' on the site.

Yet the mass arrival of people in Chios is not new. An estimated forty thousand Anatolian Greeks fled to Chios from Çeşme following the massacres carried out against them in Turkey in 1922.[1] Well over half the current population of Chios is descended from those refugees. Activists from local solidarity groups cannot make the point often enough: the history of the island and the region has been one of circular movements of people, crossing and re-crossing the Aegean for trade or empire. Now, turning in on itself, Europe has closed a border that in some ways never existed.

In the context of this denial both of history and of progress, concepts of familiarity and of return gain significance, become problematic. In Chios, a local anarchist theatre group is adapting the ancient Greek tragedies. Led by a director with an avowed love of Beckett and Ionesco, the production splices the great monologues of Greek tragic heroines with flashes of abstract film and clips from Chios's past and present. Meanwhile, *Queens of Syria*, a remarkable performance of Euripides's *Trojan Women* by refugees living in Jordan, has been touring Britain.

Very different in style, both productions seek relevance or continuity in situations where what is appropriate and what can be trusted may seem lost. Imad, who would return to Syria were it not for his nephew in Germany, claims such plays will change nothing: 'The world has seen this before, but we have not learned.' But then he adds, again with that disconcerting assurance, 'In Syria, at least we know we will die. Here, we know nothing. The world has seen before what Europe can do, but not like this. Not like this, believe me.'

---

1 http://www.irr.org.uk/news/cruelty-and-care-in-chios-greece

---

Letter from Wales

SAM ADAMS

IT IS FIFTY YEARS since we came back to Wales. Work took us to Bristol for a spell and work brought us back – though not to the mining valleys, which we called and, in unguarded moments still call, home. That's the pull, the powerful undertow, dragging you back to origins, which the Welsh call *hiraeth*. While we lived in Bristol, holidays were spent in Gilfach Goch. In the early days of exile, we even went back at weekends. It was not far by train. If you went to Stapleton Road Station at about five-thirty on a Friday evening during a school term you would find scores of Welsh teachers waiting for the train to take them 'home'. The time came when we had a car and drove across the border. It was a lengthy journey, up the east side of the Severn estuary to Gloucester for the first available bridge over the river and down the west side as far as Chepstow, where you could at last head homewards.

Or you could risk the Aust ferry which, if your luck held, would carry you across the Severn to Chepstow and save you sixty miles by road. This was a deplorable alternative that operated only when the tide was amenable. The Severn is a force of nature and there is little you can do about it; the crew of the ferry on the other hand, long familiar with the vagaries of the crossing, could have been informative about conditions on the estuary, but in our experience were peculiarly uncommunicative. At a push, the ferry's open deck would accommodate seventeen cars. There was no explanatory notice; you learned it by counting them on and off. You also counted the number of cars ahead of you to calculate how many crossings you would have to wait before your turn arrived. You might queue two hours or more and then be turned away without a word of apology or regret.

In our last couple of years in Bristol, whenever we waited at Aust hoping to catch the ferry, we would observe building activity only a short distance upstream and the gradual emergence of the two great towers of a suspension bridge. In August 1966, with our meagre array of goods and chattels going the long way in the lorry, we braved the waters of the Severn for the last time. On 9 September, the Severn Bridge opened to traffic, the M4 rolled onwards into Wales and a new era in road transport began. The ferry became instantly redundant. The Labour Minister of Transport announced compensation of £90,000 would be paid to the ferry owners. Feeling no nostalgia for this vanished institution, I would not have awarded them a penny.

Aust is said to be the location of the second, climactic meeting between Augustine, subsequently first archbishop of Canterbury, and the bishops of the Celtic church. About AD 600, Augustine, a Benedictine monk, was sent to Britain by the Pope (Gregory the Great) to convert the heathen English. He hoped to enlist the help of the Welsh, Christianised three centuries before, in the later stages of the Roman Empire. The meeting at Aust was intended to smooth ruffled feathers and align the practices of the Celtic church and those of Rome, with particular reference to the date of Easter, but also in the matter of tonsure design. Bede tells how the British bishops asked an anchorite living nearby whether they should surrender their ancient traditions at Augustine's request. The holy man answered (in Thomas Stapleton's 1565 translation of Bede's Latin), 'if he be a man of God, folow him. But how shall we prove (sayd they) that he is a man of God? The Anchoret answered: our Lord sayeth, *take ye on yow my yooke, and lerne ye of me. For I am milde, and humble of harte.* Yf therefore this Austin be milde, and humble of harte, it is likely that him selfe beareth the yooke of Christ, and will offer you the same to beare. But if he be curst, and proude, it is certaine, that he is not of God, neither must we esteme his wordes.'

But, the bishops persisted, how will we know he is humble of heart. The anchorite proposed they should ensure Augustine and his entourage entered the meeting-place first – 'And if when ye appproche nere, he ariseth courteously to you, thinke ye that he is the servant of Christe, and so heare ye him obediently. But if he despise yow, nor will vouchesafe to rise at your presence [...] let him likewise be despised of yowe.' A simple enough test, which Augustine failed: he remained seated and the bishops were convinced he held them in contempt. Emollient words did nothing to change their minds, nor did the more pressing argument that, if the English remained unconverted, in their brutal heathen way they would surely fall upon the British, persecute and vanquish them. Thus Bede brought together what he had gathered from Gildas concerning 'the ruin and conquest of Britain' and propaganda on behalf of the English church and the Papacy.

Barely two months after our return to South Wales, the Aberfan disaster brought a sickening reminder of the price of coal. Anyone brought up in the coalfield before, in the aftermath of the tragedy, all the tips were modified or swept away, will have strong personal images of the vast heaps of colliery waste that hung over the valleys. They were too much a part of existence to be considered threatening. As children in Gilfach Goch, we viewed with amused indifference the road we walked to school where fissures would open emitting wisps of smoke and where, on damp days, the air stank of combustion. It had been built over a smouldering tip. Houses and Gilfach's first school were hidden beneath another tip, but their burial had been planned and was slow. What happened at Aberfan, soon after the commencement of morning lessons on 21 October 1966, was catastrophically sudden. A black avalanche of slurry and stony debris smashed into Pantglas Junior School and nearby houses in its path, killing 116 children and 28 adults. The engulfing slide had been anticipated and feared by a few, because they knew tipping had proceeded for decades over a small stream and mountain springs. Their voices had gone unheeded and no action was taken. Individual tragedies and disasters had occurred in the coalfield before, hundreds of them, but confined to the underground workings and surface of countless collieries. This time, a generation of the children of a typical mining village were killed. In the enquiry that followed, the National Coal Board and its chairman, Lord Robens, did their best to exculpate themselves. They did not succeed, but revisiting the disaster on this fiftieth anniversary has reawakened grievances over the way the media, the Charity Commission and government bodies responded in its aftermath.

Earlier this year, I met on separate occasions two men, one in the RAF at the time, the other a collier in another valley, who had helped to dig out victims of the disaster. It haunts them still. A boyhood friend of poet and short-story writer Leslie Norris (born in Merthyr Tydfil, a few miles from Aberfan) was deputy head at the school. He and his entire class were killed. When his body was recovered he was found to have spread his arms protectively over five of his pupils as the black tide struck. In his 'Elegy for David Beynon', helpless to express the magnitude of the calamity, Leslie recalled his friend in terms of utmost simplicity:

I think those children, those who died
under your arms in the crushed school,

would understand that I make this
your elegy. I know the face you had,
have walked with you enough mornings
under the falling leaves. Theirs is

the great anonymous tragedy one word
will summarise. Aberfan, I write it
for them here, knowing we've paid to it
our shabby pence, and now it can be stored

with whatever names there are where
children end their briefest pilgrimage.
I cannot find the words for you, David. These
are too long, too many, and not enough.

From the Archive

Issue 133, May–June 2000

EDWIN MORGAN

———————————

From a contribution of two poems that also included 'Gilgamesh and Ziusura', accompanied by a conversation with Marshall Walker. Elsewhere in the issue Jody Allen Randolph is in conversation with Eavan Boland, and there are poems by Thomas Kinsella, Roger Garfitt, Sinéad Morrissey, Les Murray, and Robert Nye, among others.

AT EIGHTY

Push the boat out, campañeros,
Push the boat out, whatever the sea.
Who says we cannot guide ourselves
through the boiling reefs, black as they are,
the enemy of us all makes sure of it!
Mariners, keep good watch always
for that last passage of blue water
we have heard of and long to reach
(no matter if we cannot, no matter!)
in our eighty-year-old timbers
leaky and patched as they are but sweet,
well seasoned with the scent of woods
long perished, serviceable still
in unarrested pungency
of salt and blistering sunlight. Out,
push it all out into the unknown!
Unknown is best, it beckons best,
like distant ships in mist, or bells
clanging ruthless from stormy buoys.

Rough Notes for One or Two Undelivered Lectures on T. S. Eliot's *Dante* (4)

F R A N K   K U P P N E R

41. A grim position to be forced into, indeed! At the heart of this, I suppose, there lies some sort of *aut Caesar aut nihil* principle at work. It's all or nothing – either 100% or stark zero – and to the extent that we cannot think ourselves into the conceptual or emotional systems that the poet himself was inhabiting and writing out of, we shall necessarily be (as it were) unwittingly filling in the blanks with inappropriate or inequivalent matter drawn from [no doubt inferior] mental systems of our own.

42. Of course, one also has the option – very commonly resorted to, I should think – of simply leaving the blanks blank and going elsewhere for one's spiritual, recreational or intellectual sustenance. There are, after all, degrees of affinity, as of so much else, and, although no-one is getting everything right all the time, even a brief investigation, done in good faith, of surface aspects lying more or less immediately to hand will usually be enough to furnish us with *some* clues to help us as we try to estimate in advance whether this particular project is likely to be worth proceeding with, or is shaping up to be something of a waste of effort. Not infallibly so, no doubt – but then: who (apart from the obvious exception) is ever infallible about anything? Is this particular example of ever more ancient articulation worth persevering with? And what then about this resonant piece of high-class rhetorical prestidigitation?

43. At which point, a few hundred deeply concerned friends, working in expert collaboration, finally manage to persuade me to abandon the unequal task of providing the Oracle's message to mere Earthlings with more coherence than it was itself willing or able to import into its sublime fabric in the first place. (Indeed, it almost disconcerts me to find that I've lingered over this single point for so unconscionably long.) However, before [it is the poisoned cup!] it is too late, let us add here a note which should certainly have been worked into the fabric earlier, but which (badly confused by the state of the world today – though I certainly don't want to use this as any sort of excuse) I somehow managed to overlook completely – whether it be an envoy, an echo, an informal summary, or a piece of gross incompetence aggravated by undead sloth.

To wit: 'It would appear that "literary appreciation" is an abstraction, and pure poetry a phantom; and that both in creation and enjoyment much always enters which is, from the point of view of "Art", irrelevant.' (A distraction often referred to, I believe, as the real world.) (*Now* he tells us!) (If only it weren't for the real world, what infinite and eternal successes our finest minds would be able to achieve!)

But then, if we limit ourselves to the real world then we'll never really get anywhere really important, will we, Captain?

44. And indeed – (a second *p.s.*) – only now do I register the disconcerting fact that, in the long, small-print note between Sections II and III of Eliot's weighty essay – the very part which gives us, near the start: 'I deny, in short, that the reader must share the beliefs of the poet in order to enjoy the poetry fully' – we find him conceding in the final paragraph: 'Actually, one probably has more pleasure in the poetry when one shares the beliefs of the poet.' (Much virtue in a 'probably'. Not to mention an 'actually'. (And always read the small print.)) Here we have a pair of what might be called Supreme Court deliverances which, to say the least, do not sit at all well with each other. (In somewhat less tentative terms: it's a spectacular piece of self-contradiction. Or might it perhaps be that such a sympathy of belief allows the reader to enjoy the poetry *even more than fully*?)

'On the other hand,' Eliot continues – for on the Lord of the Ocean surges, scarcely allowing his dignified course to be much deflected by a mere harpoon or two – 'there is a distinct pleasure in enjoying poetry as poetry when one does *not* share the beliefs, analogous to the pleasure of "mastering" other men's philosophical systems.'

'Analogous', eh? I must say this sounds to me like, at best, a highly *indistinct* pleasure. Perhaps a rather more salient comparison would be the unquestionably interesting suggestion that one could enjoy other men's philosophical systems – not to say, receive communications from them – before one had even understood them. And certain it is (in a world where so little is truly certain) that to finally grasp (at last!) what a philosopher is actually saying (if indeed anything is specifically being said at all) can be a distinctly deflating type of breakthrough – but the exhausted tracker is by now terminally reluctant to be lured off further across the path into this quite different part of the woods. (Certainly not so late in the day.)

Besides which, these points may, for all I know, be the routine commonplaces of past commentary on Eliot's *Dante*, propounded and rebutted into the ground, sacred or otherwise, over the last eighty-odd years. If so, my bucolic and badly under-researched apologies. I shall now leave this particular thicket – no doubt, not before time – with the dying-fall suggestion that the pleasure of finally managing to work out that what some fine mind is attempting to convey, however beautifully, is wrong, or is more wrong than right, or has been left (perhaps with exquisite artistry) undecidable, is at best a very *precarious* pleasure, particularly if one can think of other things that were better worth doing with one's limited and ever-dwindling resources of time and energy.

Shantih, etc. etc. No offence. Keep of the grass.

Five Poems

ZOHAR ATKINS

The Binding of Isaac

Twenty minutes away, a young Muslim is dying of bone cancer
In an Israeli hospital. His sister refuses to donate her marrow
And the young man cries out in darkness, '*Allah*, Merciful One, I know
You are punishing me for all those naked women I visited.'
And under his rage is the sadness of tank-ploughed olive groves.
We read about it in our seminar and debate the pros and cons
Of hugging him. We refer to human touch as an *intervention*.
'Who are you to love me?' We hear our fantasies shout back at us.
And so it was that Abraham, having heard the angel's voice
And felt her tears, untied his only son, saying, 'God has provided
The offering for us.' But Ishmael insisted Avraham had heard wrong
And said, 'My place is here, on the altar.' And Abraham said, 'Isaac, Isaac.'
And Ishmael said, '*Hineini*.'

Seeker's Psalm

And Dinah, daughter of Leah,
little girl of Jacob, went out to look
upon the daughters of the land.
(Gen. 38:4)

Our God and God of our ancestors,
have we not also gone out to find ourselves
amongst the peoples of the world?

Have we not also left our parents' homes
in search of old questions and new light?

What was Dinah seeking when she was seen
by Shechem ben Hamor?

What image of you formed in her eyes
before she was taken by him –
taken first by force and then by love?

God who lifts mountains
over us
so we may accept your shadow

God who mines order from chaos
music from noise
struggle from conformity

God who leads us
astray
to a place we will show you

Keep us as you kept Dinah –
in the palace of Shechem

so even here
far from our origins
we may stay
Yisrael

Déjà Vu

Tell me the absence of helicopters, there
In winter blue, above the bridge, isn't

Significant – that the upside-down sign
Advertising a world at No Additional Fees

Isn't meant to draw us into it.
And poems, tell me the years don't spread,

Vainly forming a notion
Of self-worth and haggling over the boundary

Between voice and desire. Tell me this need
To hibernate isn't language's way of teasing

Forth from refusal. Tell me this staff, this rock,
This comma, projected into bread and blessing

Doesn't tell us everything we need to know to morph,
To ward, to throw unknowable music: Fire, child of snow

And snow, child of gaze. Whose? Yes. That's the point,
O chaos. So may the target of our senses and the backlog

Of our failures be acceptable to our lives that we may live
Beyond allure. Let those orange suede boots traipsing across

Your poem not dissolve your knowledge that you manifested
From a rat's periphery. She wants to be a co-author with you,

As if you were the same as you. As if the you deciding which
Words deserve to arrive – here – were not an effect of the words

They only seem to chaperone. Tell me a truth that doesn't
Reference Heidegger, a love whose knowledge exceeds all scope.

Descent

And Joseph saw his brothers, and knew them
And made himself strange to them
And spoke roughly to them.
(Genesis 42:7)

He made himself strange to them.
We might think this means he hid himself

But commentaries, rescued by chance
From the offal of Fallujah, and sold

On the Black Market to Collectors
From Hebrew U, tell otherwise.

At Tel Aviv, they say this is a fiction,
That the site of rescue was Leipzig, 1939.

There are wonders not even the human heart can save.
Can you imagine the entire Talmud

Burnt forever? Can you imagine not having heard
Of anything you assume makes a world?

Tree, stone, earth? 'It was his very strangeness
That he hoped would out him,' says Rashbam.

As if Joseph still needs us to see he's truly Joseph,
And not Pharaoh's double,

The guy Pharaoh will forget.
Joseph remembers who he is.

He is the only character in the Bible who weeps seven times,
Once for each day of Creation.

We thought we'd traded Joseph in for a life free of disturbance.
Now he sells us corn, but won't take our money.

Like the kid who keeps the Monopoly game going after he's won
By doling out handouts from the bank so his mom can keep paying him.

Meanwhile, the socialists picket, 'Where is Zebulon's chapter, and Naftali's
and Yisasschar's, and Gad's?' If only Benjamin could have lived a year longer,

Just to have written an essay redeeming the hanged baker.
We might have read theories suggesting

Dream interpretation was then what consulting is now.
Joseph was just looking at the numbers.

Dear Guru

Dear Guru,
source of ideation and aesthetically tested angst,
maker of all things your consumers pronounce
enlightened,
you who are beyond subject
and, let's not kid ourselves, object,
you who are the whoopy cushion of all metaphors,
and for whom it is a sin to even say you are,
forgive me for calling on you for such a small favour,
I know you are very busy, holding on the line
with Verizon customer service. But
I do not know how to write poetry, guru.
Teach me your ways that my words
may one day ally themselves with words
that are not mine, so the language will not mock me
or bamboozle me or take me for a ride or what
have you, so I will not be the butt of language's
cigarette anthropologists stomp on during their
lunch break. Dear guru, rescue me from the belly
of truth, in whose mouth I threw myself to hide
from you. Send me back to the Nineveh of ordinary
language, where sandwich wrappers are just
sandwich wrappers and eulogies consist entirely
of emojis. Guru, give me the wisdom you told me
I already have, if only I would lose five pounds,
or my obsession with losing weight, or my thought
or my hunger for knowledge and metaphor
and footnotes. The wisdom to stop calling
on you at such late hours. Or the wisdom to
stop calling you by your title or your middle name
(Kony? Ted? Usurpulus?) and start calling
you by your last name, which is guru
spelled backwards: urug, if only
I could pronounce it.

Xi Chuan and the Contradictory Aesthetics of Revolution

STEPHEN PROCTER

FOREIGN VISITORS TO CHINESE parks are often struck by the communal activities taking place in them. Retirees gather to practise taijiquan and traditional martial arts, they dance to folk music, and they sing patriotic songs.

It is also common for groups of dancing pensioners to gather in the public spaces in and around residential areas. While to the passing outsider this might offer a charming insight onto the national cultural life, the behaviour has come to be regarded by many Chinese people with wariness and scepticism. Clashes between the revellers and local residents, who have been driven to despair by the loud music interrupting their lives night after night, have often been reported by the media. China's Eastern cities are so densely populated that any available piece of open ground becomes a potential meeting place, regardless of the feelings of those who live nearby. On occasion requests that the dancers move to another location have led to fights. Police called in to reason with them have been chased away. One fed-up resident resorted to shooting an air rifle into the crowd, while others have thrown excrement.

Given the huge population of China, it is surprising that disputes are not more frequent. In fact Chinese people are enormously tolerant of the actions of others in public spaces, avoiding conflicts in all but the most extreme cases. Still, the herd-like behaviour of the elderly, and their insistence on their right to enjoy themselves at the cost of others' peace, have led many to question the cause of their intransigence. According to one popular joke, the explanation is not that the old are getting bad, but that the bad are getting old.

This refers, of course, to the fact that those presently entering retirement are precisely the generation who grew up during the Cultural Revolution. Many, deprived of education and stirred up by Mao's provocations, became red guards, and tore around China destroying ancient monuments and cultural artefacts, subjecting perceived counter-revolutionaries to public and often violent struggles, and engaging in ideologically motivated street battles with rival gangs.

This generation holds an uneasy position within Chinese society, being both the victims and the perpetrators of the social upheaval of the times. They have behaved destructively, but they are also a generation of extraordinary resilience whose capacity for hard work has been the key to China's economic growth. Although it is now possible to publicly discuss the harm caused during the Cultural Revolution, proper redress is made impossible by the threat it poses to the Communist Party, which holds ultimate responsibility for what happened. Some commentators draw a parallel between the gang mentality of the red guards and modern pensioners. They say that members of the older generation feel a continuing need to be part of a group, because the experiences of their youth have led them to feel vindicated and secure only in the protection of the crowd. Their urge to behave collectively is entrenched, even at the cost of the wider collective.

The Cultural Revolution not only continues to influence the social relations of those who lived through it, but also explains and taints much that is taking place in contemporary politics. It is no accident that, since the deaths of Mao Zedong and Zhou Enlai in 1976, many of China's most important leaders, from Deng Xiaoping to today's party general secretary Xi Jinping, were themselves victims of persecution in the Cultural Revolution. That the fortieth anniversary of Mao's death was marked in 2016 with only muted fanfare reflects the uneasiness of the former leader's place in modern China. Although his rounded, fatherly face remains ubiquitous, from banknotes to the huge portrait occupying the focal position in Tiananmen Square, the political authorities are opposed to the extreme leftism of the 1960s and 1970s, and anxious about the possibility of further upheavals driven by widespread social movements. It is this paranoia, fuelled further by fears about the 'new normal' of economic slowdown, which goes much of the way to explaining the increasing autocracy of Xi's regime.

*

Xi Chuan (whose name is written with a different character to the family name of his country's leader) was born in 1964, and therefore spent most of his earliest years in the midst of the Cultural Revolution. His adolescence and early adulthood were passed in that fruitful period for Chinese art sandwiched between 1976 and 1989, when restrictions on social freedoms were falling away and many were optimistic about the future.

The early work that he produced, like that of his contemporaries, reflects a society undergoing change. In his poems of this period the dominant mood is loneliness ('each day a person disappears from the earth', 'nobody but me / could be planning to pass beneath this bridge', 'The city I live in has no people', 'I know what it means to be lonely'), the time of day is dusk ('the sunset in the *hutong* street cast a shadow', 'in the vast expanse of a nation / Twilight is equally vast', 'excess dusk presses onto my tent', 'Darkness approaches'), the season is autumn ('The curtain of autumn falls with a thud', 'September comes', 'Autumn over the land'), and the place is on the margins of the urban environment. It is a world in transition (from light to dark, summer to winter, urban to rural); and yet it is curiously unchanging, because of the repetition of the same state from poem to poem. In this respect there is a resemblance to the paintings of Giorgio de Chirico, which show again and again a cityscape bisected by long shadows, in which the signs of human activity have been pushed to the margins, leaving the viewer in melancholy solitude, contemplating the empty space at the heart of the scene. These paintings likewise capture flux in a paradoxically static state, revealing a frozen world of encroaching shadow, a movement from the timeless to the measured, from the traditional to the modern.

Xi Chuan perhaps best intertwines these themes in the poem 'Three Chapters on Dusk', where change and repetition are combined more self-consciously: 'the setting sun repeats itself [...] this is the eighth dusk of autumn'. Here, as the city fragments, entropy is suggested: 'plains push out from the edge of the city / mountains lift up at the edge of the plains'. Chance, rather than organisation, is emphasised, and Lucas Klein (his English translator) skilfully renders the repetitious means through which this is conveyed:

I see aberrant turrets, lamps, and squares
as if I'd only happened on this evening
a happening of people running through a meadow, a hap-
     penstance mindset
hearing a blind man's haphazard fiddle

At the poem's conclusion, 'we' become subject to the transition that is taking place: 'we become history / that page has to be turned'. The accumulated transitions finally crystallise here into historical anticipation. Caught between epochs, the Cultural Revolution and the emerging capitalism of Deng Xia-oping's 'socialism with Chinese characteristics', the world of the early poems is one where something, somehow, is about to happen...

*

The anticipated future finally became concrete reality for Xi Chuan, as it did for all of the country's hopeful youth, in the calamitous year of 1989, when illusions were shattered and the precise shape of China's destiny became tangible reality. This year of tragedy – for Xi Chuan personal as well as national, as he saw close friends become victims – proved a turning point. The idealism, or abstraction, of the 1980s had to give way to something more solid, more visceral, and more urgent. Xi Chuan sensed this more than anyone else, and after a hiatus provoked by the events of 1989 he returned a transformed artist.

How far Xi Chuan had come can be seen in a single poem, 'Written at Thirty', a kind of condensed *Bildungsroman* in which the poet surveys his development over the preceding three decades. Thirty, accord-ing to Confucian tradition, is the age at which a man ought to give up his youthful meanderings and make a place for himself in society. In addition to taking stock of his own past, Xi Chuan interrogates the social environment into which he has emerged. His 'first decade', which coincides with the Cultural Revolu-tion, witnesses 'a clatter of exorcismal gongs and shouts in the street', presumably the purging of class enemies in a public procession. There is an implied loss of innocence in these early experiences ('a girl pulled down her pants in front of me / I ran into a suicide's shade on the stairs'), and yet the ghostly language with which they are described lends them an unreality, making the question of responsibility

more ambiguous, and preventing the poem from being confessional in a conventional sense. When he says that he and his contemporaries 'together fell in love with violence and moonlight', does it mean that they acted violently, or is it a more commonplace boyhood attraction to toy guns and war games?

As he grows in the poem, sexuality and violence continue to intermingle in 'riots of flesh that called forth rainstorms', but the language shifts gradu-ally from the spectral to the physical ('no faerie queens descend on the streets'). There is a stanza for each of the decades of his life, followed by a fourth and final one in which the preceding violence and guilt condense as he looks to the future:

how can you doubt both yourself and the world at once?
you can't stop the rain, can't get a bird to land in your hand
thought's like a knife, a flick of the blade
drenches my spirit in sweat
I drive out thirty contentious philosophers
and say to the shadow who guards me, *I'm sorry*
salty sweat, salty tears, what else is flesh supposed to taste
     like?
night is like a display of identical rooms
I walk through, pacing
back and forth as if it were all one room. Morning to night
my worries for the future prove I'm ill at ease—
the earth is in motion but I have yet to sense it—

Here Xi Chuan not only confronts himself, history, and a changing world, but also discovers a language of contradiction apposite for their description. This new mode, at once immediate and paradox-ical, is prominent in his subsequent poems.

*

One ought to be more precise, as is Xi Chuan him-self, by making a distinction between contradiction and oxymoron:

Some thirty years ago, people said that in China 'left is right and right is wrong.' And now, to live in the shadow of oxymoron means to live in embarrassment; it means to enjoy absurd happiness. Yet to speak in oxymorons means that you are a person who is not understandable. I am not using words like 'contradiction,' because contradictions are to be blended and eventually dissolved, whereas the social oxymoron is the reality.[1]

While potentially a contradiction might be logically fertile, assisting in the discovery of meaning, the indissolubility of the oxymoron must simply be accepted, with no meaning being made to adhere to it. As Xi Chuan points out, the latter pervade contem-porary discourse, in phrases such as 'party-member capitalist' and 'Socialist Market Economy', and they are the linguistic legacy of the early days of commu-nist China, which proclaimed the 'People's Demo-cratic Dictatorship'. According to Xi Chuan, Chinese literary tradition is not just a matter of immersion

---

1 Xi Chuan, 'In the Shadow of Oxymoron', *91st Meridian* (7.2, autumn 2011).

in the classics, but also of coming to terms with the 'minor tradition' of socialism which has played its own role in shaping the language.

Xi Chuan's writings reflect the dual capacity of oxymoron to act both as a tool to sharpen thought and as a blunt instrument recording its failure; as, for example, in the poem 'I Bury My Tail':

If others repeat my foolish mistakes, I can't stop them. If I repeat them, it's to show my cunning.

Can't stand by the mad with hands tied by the evil of the sane, and can't stand by the sane with hands tied by the evils of the mad.

Here is the contemporary language of illogic, but also a quasi-Marxist positioning of antithetical propositions. The significance of contradiction, on the other hand, has much deeper roots in Chinese thought, featuring in Daoist philosophy as exemplified by Laozi and Zhuangzi. One of their characteristic devices is to take a commonplace idea – such as that 'hard and strong' are inherently superior to their respective opposites – and to subvert it by revealing the opposite to be the case – that they will be surpassed by the 'soft and tender':

When alive, man is soft and tender
After death, he is hard and stiff...
All things like grass and trees are soft and tender when alive,
Whereas they become withered and dried when dead.
Therefore, the hard and stiff are companions of death
Whereas the soft and tender are companions of life.
Hence an army will be shattered when it becomes strong.
A tree will be broken when it grows huge.
The hard and strong fall in the inferior position;
The soft and tender stay in the superior position.
'The violent and strong do not die natural deaths.'
I shall take this principle as the father of my teaching.
(*Laozi*, 76)

The goal of this kind of reasoning is not obscurity, but to establish a productive dialectic between irreconcilable modes of thought. This more reasonable legacy of contradiction also finds a place in Xi Chuan's poems, where contradiction is not merely a satire of political jargon. Indeed, a taxonomy of contradiction is needed to describe a poet capable of so deftly walking the line between foolish wisdom and wise foolishness.

This line might be understood as a form of resistance: not just to the pressures of the native political mainstream, but also to expectations from outside that in an autocracy the only true literature must be in the form of dissidence. It is characteristic in Western Europe and North America, especially among certain members of the older generation, to take the view that a writer must be strictly for or against. This binary way of thinking is surely a legacy of the Cold War, and it was noticeable, for example, in Salman Rushdie's demand that Mo Yan publicly denounce the Chinese Communist Party. It seemed puzzling that Mo Yan might write novels drawing attention to the disastrous consequences of communist policy while continuing to maintain his affection for his former employer, the People's Liberation Army, a primary pillar of the hegemony. We are accustomed to believing that all of our actions and utterances bear social and political responsibility. This may be the case, but our insistence upon the principle blinds us to the existence of a parallel world in which this way of thinking has been less dominant. Daoism partly has its origins in the philosophers of the Warring States period who, as the Sinologist Joseph Needham writes in his *Science & Civilisation in China*, 'followed a Tao of Nature rather than a Tao of Human Society, who did not want to be employed by the feudal princes, and who withdrew into the countryside or the wilderness to meditate and study Nature'. Throughout Chinese history, and following the influence of Daoism, in times of political tyranny intellectuals have withdrawn from the centre to a life of simplicity and solitude on the peripheries. I do not claim that Xi Chuan has made such a retreat – indeed, he is ill at ease with what he calls 'absentee landlord' culture, which observes cynically from outside, detaching itself from reality. But this tradition partly explains his reluctance to sacrifice his autonomy on one or the other side. It also illuminates his fascination with the intellectual margins, the esoteric, 'the ancient culture of strange gods, mysterious forces, trickster witchcraft, alien Buddhism, and aphrodisiacs'.[2]

*

Xi Chuan's prioritisation of the extremities of Chinese culture – what we might call his eccentricity – results partly from the complicated relationship between tradition and the mainstream. As the world changes, so its aesthetic experiences alter. Those which have previously been held up as iconic no longer possess the potency they once did – naturally, since the conditions which produced them are no longer present. Xi Chuan takes Li Bai's poems of 'The Autumn Shores', canonical texts on a quintessentially Chinese landscape, as examples. On visiting Chizhou, the site of their composition, Xi Chuan felt only a sense of deflation: 'Imagine my embarrassment when, facing the stillness of the river as it blended with dusk at the tourist site of the Autumn Shores Fishing Village, I was unable to assume Li Bai's state of mind.'[3] Not only the sentiments which provoked the original experience, but also the context for their modern appreciation, have shifted in orientation. The same displacement of sensibility reappears in the poems, particularly in the sequence *Senses of Reality*: 'I'm no longer a little kid, so do I still have to jump for joy at the moon over the Eastern mountain?' 'Green mountains and sky-blue water, there's too much of it. / Gazing at the magnificent mountains, I ended up falling asleep.' The point, however, is not to mourn the loss of a sensation whose currency has diminished. Instead Xi Chuan deviously forges a new aesthetic, its divergence from the expected norm becoming a source of pride:

---

2 Xi Chuan, 'The Tradition This Instant', Author's Afterword to *Notes on the Mosquito: Selected Poems*, translated by Lucas Klein (New Directions, 2012).
3 *Ibid.*

For no good reason they kept hiking after we decided to
   stop.
We decided to leave them the limitless scenery of the peak:
   leave them to be stupefied.
We decided to give ourselves a bit of regret, to make an
   appearance at the boulder halfway up the mountain.
[...]
We are in love with our decision; when they come down
   they'll be stupefied.

Neither is the purpose to assert the demise of
tradition; instead what is signalled is its relocation
– as much geographical as ideological – away from
the historical heartland. Xi Chuan's conception of
tradition is less monocultural, less Han-centric,
more open to outside influence, and more at ease
with contradiction and inconsistency.

   Xi Chuan reflects the way in which the margins
feed into the centre. As he points out, marginal
annotation is the primary means through which
Chinese culture has been transmitted. In 'That
Person Writing', it is the unnamed ancient scribe
whose modifications flow into the mainstream:
'Wittingly or not certain words are altered, wit-
tingly or not he retains his own breath within the
views of another. From a humble stenographer, he
unwittingly transforms into a minor author, like an
ant tethering thought's kite against the wind.' By
focusing only on the central currents, we miss the
process of accumulation through which a culture
comes into being, its essential force. The life of
tradition is in its transmission, not its preservation:

An antique shop on Jadestream Road in Dali's old quarter.
A gray-green brick in the shop from the late Nanzhao era.
On the gray-green brick eleven lines of Sanskrit. The hands
that molded the Sanskrit lines. The hands that inlaid the
brick into the base of the pagoda. The late Nanzhao monk
who could read the eleven lines of Sanskrit. The man or
men who brought Sanskrit from India through Nepal to
Nanzhao. ('A Sanskrit Brick from the Nanzhao Kingdom
(738–937CE)')

Transmission is haphazard. It cuts across bound-
aries. Neither its end nor its means remain con-
stant. Still, it retains a kind of eternal presence.

                              *

Where exactly are we to place a poet so resistant
to circumscription as Xi Chuan? To some extent
he stands in the same relation to his predecessors,
the 'Misty' or 'Obscure' poets, as the filmmaker Jia
Zhangke does to the 'Fifth Generation' directors,
who included Zhang Yimou and Chen Kaige. Like Jia
Zhangke (in whose early film *Platform* he acted), Xi
Chuan is the successor to a movement that cap-
tured international attention and signified China's
artistic renewal following the Cultural Revolution,
but cannot himself be straightforwardly slotted
into any obvious grouping. Is their non-affiliation
to be taken as a sign of independence or of apathy,
resilience or resignation? It is probably unhelpful to
over-emphasise the connection between these two
artists, but it can be seen that both filmmaker and

poet have sought out a new aesthetic which not only
responds to, but ambitiously tries to reshape, the
tradition from which it has emerged. In the case of
Jia Zhangke this has been expressed in a blurring
of the division between fiction and documentary in
order to reflect the social upheavals of a globalised
economy. Though the results are quite different,
Xi Chuan's has also developed from the necessity
of being truthful to a changing reality. In his own
words:

All social contradictions, paradoxes and oxymorons may
lead to a way of thinking and eventually make a language.
During the last three decades, China changed a lot.
Before that, there was the Cultural Revolution. I grew
up in and after the revolution and was thrown into its
mayhems and turbulences. And after the revolution I find
myself peddling a kind of so-called self-colored social-
ism. The way in front of me is not from A to B, but from
A to X. It makes me need new ideas, new images and new
syntaxes. By and by, what I have learnt from previous
writers and poets, their schools and isms, regardless
of whether they were Chinese or not, is not sufficient
any more. It seems to me that history and reality are
themselves inventing a kind of literature. To be honest
to oneself means to be loyal to your sense of reality. You
don't need to mirror that reality, but you need to be sym-
metrical to the vigor of history and of reality. (Xi Chuan,
'Style Comes as a Reward', *Almost Island*, winter 2012)

J. H. Prynne in China

DIANA BRIDGE

i.

To begin with, you were on your own. Down
the rabbit hole, ideas welling; the fun, the fear of that.
From one word to another, as the gifted child saw,
was rowing between islands. Two or more
islands were cranes, fishing companionably close.
No special pattern to cranes. But feed in, not setting
but space, as the Chinese know space, and one day
the islands rise in a spray of swallows, godwits headed
for the far rim of the earth. Readable, after a fashion.

Then came the time when you opened an index and
found there were two. Manichaean, then, the Chinese word?
No, nothing like that, just two arms of the track
they employ for hunting it down. You land
on the radical first. Oblique as a held spear,
quivering in shafts of live fur or disclosing
the balance inherent in wood, etching a shoulder
of roof. Meaning and mimicry blent
in a shower of dots.
                                        You cross to part two.
Strokes line up by number under each root.
Brief units of sense, of sound, incoherent on their own.
To break open before you rebuild –
does that ring a bell? Fifteen strokes and counting.
The fragment glitters into not-quite-meaning
before the left side reaches out a hand
and there's the sparkle of ignition. So, is this
where you got it, your passion for syntax undone?

ii.

Words start in an underworld, its byways ready to be mined.
Those at home in the dusty tunnels of old texts discover
webs of origin. Endlessly paraded, the sources:
historical and legendary, cautionary, inspiring.
It's how you draw them out. Allusion shines its light
from the side. Examples only seem to strengthen.
Driven to re-invent, the best push on the door.
Du Fu did it, drunk with indignation, mad
with a fire that undoes structure. Lines

splinter under their load. Never a time when words
don't fracture. They fissure on the rack of politics.
No such thing as tense. It's true. Only last century,
small red-guard words disrupting everything. Revolution
carried too far. (But do we want what followed? Across
our planet calculation yields a crooked history.)
Mao was surely and severely wrong, but nonetheless
knew this. From contradictions arise new patches
of map. Grasp and apply. You take him up.

And then it rains, blotting out hardly the sun; there was never
much brightness. What is left? Young untried outlines.
Remember, from one word to another is rowing between
islands. Neither word new, nor brave, but together –
I know how this sounds – a universe, then. You,
as always, on the brink. We give ourselves to contiguity.
And the payoff? In the humdrum branches, in lieu
of revelation, are lumps of catch-your-breath
crystal. No more handholds. Just let go.

'All That Needs to Be and Nothing Else'

An Appreciation of Michael Hersch

MARIUS KOCIEJOWSKI

16–17
Poems
Bridge
Features
Kociejowski
& Hersch

THE OTHER NIGHT I went to a performance of Leoš Janáček's *Jenůfa*. I wonder if ever there was an opera that so brutally wrenches one from hell to purgatory and onward to uncertain paradise. Dostoevsky could have written the libretto, Sophocles might have staged it, Janáček most definitely composed it. I defy anyone not to be emotionally drained by the ride. One of its great ironies is that the music is never more sublime than at the moment of greatest horror. There is, finally, a species of happiness to be had, though it will have to be shared with snoopy neighbours who are a kind of hell in themselves. As with Greek tragedy, the darkest and the most hopeless in all literature, the opera does not leave one feeling depressed: Janáček takes his music not only through but *above* human suffering. My heart in a sling, my brain elsewhere, I left the opera house without my glasses. I rushed back and was told they'd been found and that I could collect them at the stage door. I got there just in time to see Jenůfa herself leave, so ordinary, so smashing, in her regular street clothes. I wanted to say something to her but couldn't. All that could be said had already been explored to the extreme in this greatest of twentieth-century operas.

The *greatest* of twentieth-century operas? *Really*? How so? What a fix music puts us in, who love it but have not the words to say how or why it percolates through to some halfway house between mind and heart. Perhaps this is no bad thing, since it is with the musically illiterate that all music has its final resting place. Academic coaxing will not get it there, nor will reduced ticket prices. This is particularly true of new music, much of which seems to be aimed at the intellect only and ignores the heart's desires. The human mind can absorb only so much cold, unresolved matter and I suspect we have been at saturation point for a while. Which is not to say I'm pining for things as they once were – I don't want to be fed stuffed toccatas, nor do I seek the powdered spirituality to which one simply adds water and stirs. And with regard to 'music for relaxation' – there is a classical radio station devoted to that ghastly premise – it induces feelings of extreme violence in me. We must continue to explore, no matter what, and even upon the most obdurate of surfaces, because if exploration comes to an end our culture will tumble. There's no getting around the fact that much new music is difficult, at least that which is of substance. What Geoffrey Hill – a difficult poet, a man who scorned easy solutions – had to say in an interview about poetry applies equally to music: 'We are difficult. Human beings are difficult. We're difficult to ourselves, we're difficult to each other. And we are mysteries to ourselves, we are mysteries to each other. One encounters in any ordinary day far more real difficulty than one confronts in the most 'intellectual' piece of work. Why is it believed that poetry, prose, painting, music should be less than we are?'

I stare helplessly, as might a primitive at a public notice, at the massive score before me, a reproduction of the composer's own final manuscript. On one of its pages the notes dangle from the staves like rows of executed human figures. Silly, I know, but this page in particular throbs with violence. *So the flashing knife will split / Memory down the middle.* Translate that, if you will, into music. On second thoughts, no. Do not translate it. Give it expression somewhere within the sonic range of the instrument that asks of one that he capture, by music alone, the dark pull of that line. Can such a thing be done? Apparently it can, with 'a stabbing chord and a plunging gesture', according to Andrew Farach-Colton's liner notes to the Vanguard Classics recording of Michael Hersch's *The Vanishing Pavilions* (2005), the expansive piano work which draws on this very American composer's reading of the poetry of the very English Christopher Middleton. It works. I'm at a loss to say *why*, but what I read in Middleton I listen to in Hersch. They are, both the poet's and the composer's lines, deeply mysterious, but to apply meaning to them could easily break the spell they create. And yet to say merely that the music *feels* right is to err on the side of cowardice. Though perhaps there is a way. Maybe I can bring to the page something of the charge that both produce in me.

The music of Michael Hersch first came to me through my friendship with the poet, whose mighty gift was to be able to pique one's interest with a mere mention of whatever excited him at the time. The greatest attribute any teacher possesses – and here I mean 'teacher' in the widest possible sense – is *enthusiasm*. Middleton had it in abundance, increasingly so with age, even though for many people life diminishes in strength with the years. So potent was that gift that twenty years ago, without intending to, he set me off on a trajectory that was to last for over a decade, and all because one day in June 1995, over fishcakes in Cambridge, he pulled from his pocket a coin from Antioch and asked me what I thought of it. Antioch, to which I'd given no thought at all, became a place I simply had to go to. Middleton's was a mind with alchemical properties and the most powerful elixir in his vocabulary was *activate. Art must seek to activate.* Yet it must do so without force. I am put in mind of W. B. Yeats when he writes of J. M. Synge, 'Only that which does not teach, which does not cry out, which does not persuade, which does not condescend, which does not explain, is irresistible.' The man who asserts too much is bound to be ignored. Christopher Middleton, who died on 29 November 2015, continues to address me, as I should think is the case with anyone fortunate enough to have met him. And because one thing sparks another, it is of another head he turned that I now write.

In the autumn of 2001, Middleton was a residential Fellow of the American Academy in Berlin. There, over breakfast, he had daily conversations with another Fellow, a shy, young American composer who would disappear into his room for hours on end to produce another bar or two of what would turn out to be his *Second Symphony*. My own experience of Christopher, as I shall now address him, was that he would come to our breakfast table fully primed with arcane knowledge. This would be tantamount to pouring lead into one's porridge were it not that he did so with an effervescence that teased the comatose brain cells to life. Actually, his and Hersch's first conversation was not at table but on a boat on Lake Wannsee, and it was about how best to translate part of a line from Hölderlin's poem '*Hälfte des Lebens*': '*im Winde / Klirren die Fahnen*'. An hour later, they settled on the version that goes 'in the wind / weathervanes clatter', which to both minds captured best the metallic sound the interaction between wind and object makes. This was not some academic exercise: they had netted each other's sensibilities. At the Academy Christopher would later act as moderator for Hersch, who gave a public presentation of his musical project. Though it was rather more than that: it was a poet speaking for a composer, speaking for his music. That exchange was to spark a revolution in the composer's mind.

M. H. composing © Sam Oberter

What was that strange music of which Christopher wrote to me? 'I think you'd be bowled over by its richness, its exploration of altogether hitherto unheard reaches of tonality.' This coming from a man who, when I played him the music that enthused me, would often say, 'That's enough' – not necessarily because he disliked it, although sometimes this really was the case, but because, somewhat to my annoyance, he preferred to absorb music in small bites. Also his was a most particular palate, much given to the light-dappled music of 'Les Six' or the Catalan composer Federico Mompou. What he wanted was music with a hint of spumescence. It was no good trying to throw Wagner at him. Opera he didn't get at all and symphonies put him in a yoke. I will hazard his snorts of derision and say that musically my friend with the hard poetical eye was a sentimentalist at heart. That he should have responded as positively as he did to the dark and tragic sonorities of Michael Hersch when he preferred to be tickled rather than bludgeoned by music is still something of a mystery to me, and it was strange, too, that a man given to small bites should have responded so to a composer who, even in his music for solo instrument, writes on an epic scale.

Christopher's enthusiasm was enough for me to order a copy of *Chamber Music* (Vanguard Classics) with Hersch himself at the piano and with other pieces performed by members of the Berlin Philharmonic. I began with the last piece, *Octet for Strings*. I'd looked at the programme notes first and saw that Hersch was inspired by his reading of Georg Trakl a number of whose poems, 'Helian' in particular, Christopher has superbly translated. The *Octet*, which draws on Trakl's poem 'Im Dorf' (In the Village), begins with thick swathes of sound, a bit like the paint Leon Kossoff applies to his canvases, whose patterns slowly emerge. This layering of sound in single bold strokes was an aspect of Hersch's music that would soon captivate me. The music moved from low to high, from morose to ecstatic. This was music I *needed*. It was music that restored my faith, which admittedly had begun to wane a little, in the new. Also this was Trakl as Trakl might have been had he turned to music rather than poetry, the anguish and visionary aspect of a deeply tormented man now faithfully rendered in pure sound. I would suggest to anyone curious about Hersch's work that he begin here, although, to be honest, what I really want is to recreate in other people my own first experience of this masterpiece. I must do so without force. When I listened to *After Hölderlin's Hälfte des Lebens* for viola and cello I realised that here was someone whose dedication to poetry was profound and that it informed his music more than any other composer I'd heard of late. (Other poets to have entered his music include Zbigniew Herbert, Czesław Miłosz, Ezra Pound, Thomas Hardy, W. G. Sebald, Jean Follain and somebody called Dante. Bruno Schulz is a rare prose presence although surely it's the poet in him who captivates.) If the *Octet* remains a favourite of mine it is not because it is necessarily Hersch's best work – he has dismissed as juvenilia much of what he wrote before 2005 and is rarely, if ever, happy with anything he pens – but because it was my point of entry into his sonic world: this was music that made me possessive of it. Also, and it's where I like music to put me, it made me feel *absolutely alone*. It is difficult too, but then why should music be less than we are?

The next work I listened to, which was the fruit of those eight months Hersch spent in Berlin, was the Naxos recording of the *Second Symphony*, performed by the Bournemouth Symphony Orchestra under the baton of Marin Alsop, a work that is both strident and elegiac. Although it would be reckless to apply a specific programme to it, its composition coincided with the shocking event of September 2001. I wonder if there is a single musical work that more accurately captures that historical moment. Where others might recoil from its dissonance, I took pleasure in its lyricism and indeed the symphony is at its most profound in its most tranquil moments. The opening assault of the symphony – and it gives one no time to prepare, no time to fasten one's mental armour – gives over to elegy, which at times becomes almost a whisper, and then, as if too much tenderness would be unbearable, there comes yet again another explosion of sound, a species of sonic rage. This running battle between the strident and the lyrical is an aspect that can be applied to the composer's *oeuvre* as a whole. When, not long ago, I tried to press the work upon a notable music critic he said, wearily, that the symphony as a form no longer has any place in modern music. Surely, though, what he meant is that the symphony is dormant only when there is no call for it, when there is nothing left to be said with it, when, in the face of too much knowledge, the epic forms curl up and die.

This is perhaps the moment to relate to the unini-

M.H. performing *The Vanishing Pavilions* © Richard Anderson

tiated something of the early days of a career that has gone from strength to strength. While it is quite true it was not until the age of eighteen that, while listening to Beethoven's Fifth, Hersch had, so to speak, an epiphany and right there and then knew he would become a composer, as explanations go this is probably a shade simplistic. We love a legend, of course, but must resist it when it becomes more important than what it describes. Numerous articles relate Hersch's meteoric development as a musician, his progression within two years from playing no piano at all to being able to perform at concert level. Within weeks of hearing the Beethoven, he had already mastered the basics of compositional theory and was writing his own music. Again, we must not allow ourselves to be seduced by the overly remarkable. We celebrate not Beethoven's deafness but his music. Soon after, Hersch was admitted to the Peabody Institute of Music and there attended a composer's workshop where he met the composer George Rochberg, who remarked on how he 'sounds the dark places of the human heart' and that, at twenty-three, 'his voice, his signature

was already unmistakably there.' At the age of twenty-five he was one of the youngest people ever to be awarded a Guggenheim Fellowship and from then on he would receive any number of prestigious prizes and fellowships, including the Berlin Prize and the Rome Prize, both before the age of thirty. There is perhaps something just a little tedious in relating a man's curriculum vitae. Maybe what impresses me more is that Hersch's *Fourteen Pieces for Unaccompanied Violin* had its world première in Janáček's house in Brno, Czech Republic. This is where music should be, in small rooms inhabited by mighty ghosts. The word 'genius' has been bandied about although I have, on occasion, heard the opposite. It is much to the composer's credit that he ignores both praise and censure.

A shade simplistic is the biography of any artist, in that the true creative life cannot be delineated. Good thing too. It's probably why I detest biopics, for their reductionism. It wasn't as if, aged eighteen, Hersch had suddenly opened his ears for the first time. He had always loved music of one kind or another – heavy metal, for example, and bluegrass – but at an early age he had already developed an antipathy for the trite. A bit of documentary evidence comes in the shape of a photograph of the young boy in anguish, covering his ears at the sound of 'Happy Birthday' being sung to him. The boy was soon to become a graduate of the slaughterhouse. As biographical anecdote goes, this ought not to be lightly dismissed. His father had a farm, deep in Appalachia, near the West Virginia border. A city man hungry for other pastures, he was in the meat trade. Hersch describes a childhood visit to a slaughterhouse: 'I have this awful memory of going with my father into one and holding his hand while being at eyelevel with the waist of the man he was talking to, who had on his belt all these different knives. The floor had about half an inch of blood across it and I remember lifting my shoes and noticing how the consistency wasn't quite like water. It was sticky.' I, too, grew up on the farm and there can be no erasing memories of the darker side of that existence. I've seen an evil bug move through a herd of cattle. I've seen a new-born calf die in my father's arms. 'One incident that upset me as a child,' Hersch continues, 'was when a cow that had just had a calf got lockjaw and there I was, looking at this baby. We had them in the barnyard and the mother was going berserk, foaming at the mouth, arching her back. She died then and there. I was convinced that calf knew what had just happened. Of course I had no idea what was going through the calf's mind, but as a small child I projected myself into the situation and considered the loss of a parent as about the most terrifying situation one could conceive of.' A childhood spent in the vicinity of the abattoir does stick to one's adulthood, and the blood seeps through into whatever one creates.

There is in much of Hersch's recent music a confrontation with bodily destruction. Some of it, such as his recent monodrama in two acts, *On the Threshold of Winter* (2012), based on the poems of the dying Marin Sorescu, draws on the composer's own struggles with cancer, and with the death of a close friend from the same disease. A similarly dark note runs through his extraordinary *Last Autumn* for Horn and Cello (2008) and *Images from a Closed Ward* for String Quartet (2010).

The music is unflinching, almost too much so at times, for there isn't any hymn of joy to be had in the release from pain, such as one finds in Beethoven's *String Quartet in A Minor* – there is, rather, a trailing off into silence. This, I believe, is the single most disturbing aspect of Hersch's music, the absence of resolution, the sure knowledge that we must all deteriorate. I suspect this is a matter he'll have to address in the next stage of his career, the fact that we are rather more than our physical selves. Suffering is not of itself resolution. Janáček, who knew a thing or two about sorrow above all things, knew this. I would not say any of this to a man of lesser talent; I write of a composer in whom my greatest hopes reside. A few years later, when I got to know him, I expressed my concerns, asking him how he goes so deep into the darkness without returning from it permanently scarred. And given that I spend so much of my own time in darkness, finding there luminous foliage, the question was a serious one. I'm not sure I ever got a straight response, although most likely it lies in the fact that the works keep coming, and that even in the face of serious illness there has been no quelling of his energies. That said, I challenge him to compose a gavotte.

What was still under wraps was the piano sonata, which Hersch describes as 'a shattered song cycle without words'. An immense work lasting two and a half hours – some fifty movements, divided into two books – *The Vanishing Pavilions*, the composer's musical exploration of the poetry of Christopher Middleton, shall be the focus of my enquiries, most specifically in the relationship between word and music. Although for Hersch it marks the beginning of his great musical enterprise, there is nothing to be taken lightly or dismissed in the music leading up to it. The poet was present at the composer's premiere on 14 October 2006 at Saint Mark's Church in Philadelphia. Hersch played the entire 339-page work from memory. I was soon to receive Christopher's reaction:

A totally 'monstrous' work! Hardly anyone else could perform it, hardly any music organisation would risk launching it? Yet there was never a dull moment … It has taken him 4 years to write, and the last of the four in transcribing the score (a very thick book). In effect, he releases from the piano possibilities unheard till now; he has altered, I'd wager, the atlas of the piano as an expressive instrument. As for the emotional range of the composition – marvellous delicate intricate notations of emotion of the darkest and most resplendent Truth – absolutely no histrionics. There's rage in it, wrenching rage, & sweetness that's surprising. Not a lot of it is tonal. But the disharmonies are exhilarating. The poor devil – he's only 35 now – and critics have already been comparing him to Beethoven and Shostakovich.

Most tellingly, in the same letter, Christopher's memory reduces the performance to about a third of its actual length. What is surprising is how, even at its most abstract, so much the music is memorable. I will not say it is hummable, but whole bars of it come back to haunt one at unexpected moments, and even what is seemingly familiar in it reveals, with each hearing, fresh discoveries. It works as only the best poetry does.

I had yet to meet Hersch. We had corresponded several times, and I wondered at the mind of a man who stapled together the pages of his letters to me. I had been warned that he was one of the most taciturn of people, a musical Samuel Beckett of sorts, given to lengthy silences. I met his wife Karen first, a classical scholar, who described to me how once in Rome, in the early days of their relationship, she found him leaning against an outside wall, a look of sheer agony in his face. Clearly some tragedy had just befallen him. What had happened was that he'd received a dinner invitation.

When he finally came to London I didn't know what to feed him or what to say. What I got was a man of hearty appetite, who spoke as if someone had pulled the stopper out of the Aswan Dam, a torrent of speech charged with boyish enthusiasm. I daresay he was even jolly at times. There seemed to be some inexplicable distance between the man and the dark tonalities of his music. And yet there is something of the pathologically shy about him. When he performs he asks that the piano be turned at an angle so that people can't observe his hands as if they were, in his words, 'some kind of scientific curiosity'. There is this need to shelter himself against outside forces, whatever they may be. With respect to his own music he was to prove, in conversation, the most generous of people, happy to field my enquiries.

What was of particular interest to me was to get his side of the story with respect to Christopher's attendance at the premiere of *The Vanishing Pavilions*, which he describes as 'one of the greatest moments of artistic terror' in his life:

Throughout those four years of composition Christopher had explicitly not asked to see what I was doing within the piece regarding his poetry. I had mentioned that apart from one poem, the poetry which companioned the music within the score was in fragments. I was initially surprised that he seemed comfortable with my doing this. I didn't know what to make of his engagement, or lack thereof. Perhaps he trusted me. Perhaps he did not care. All I knew was that an artist far greater than I seemed to be providing the space for his words to co-exist with music without standing over my shoulder. Over the first year of my work on the piece I would periodically inquire if he would like to see how his words figured into the score. He never really responded directly, so I stopped asking. Okay, I thought, I'm just going to do this. Over the next few years I went on to complete the piece without having shown or performed any of it for him. The evening before the première in Philadelphia I remember sitting in the lobby of the hotel where he was staying. Christopher has just given me this wonderful gift, a binder that his father had used for choral music [when he was music master at St John's College, Cambridge]. I then presented him a copy of the score for the first time, which included all the accompanying texts. He sat there for what seemed an eternity. After some time he smiled, rose, and patted me on the back. He seemed happy. On some level I think he was simply intrigued to see his poetry distilled in this way. It was not that I had done anything special, far from it. It was that these fragments allowed him to, possibly, see his work through another prism. We never really spoke of it again.

I wondered at how the reading of words on a page,

especially when broken down into fragments, could translate into musical expression. When I put this to Hersch he was most succinct on the matter:

It's a strange process to try and explain, but because I love literature so much, especially poetry, I have lots of it swimming around in my mind in a kind of near-constant hum. Human minds are complicated things, obviously, with many component parts, and these parts feel to me very much like distinct compartments. I can almost feel them as if they were spaces within a house. My love of poetry breaks sometimes into the abstract musical spaces where I compose. The words can then become something like companions. Even though I'm not usually setting the text to be audibly communicated, the text and music begin to bleed together in my mind. It's as if the words become tangled up in the notes, in the rests, bars, and beams ... the words get stuck inside there and it becomes difficult to extract them. They – the music and the text – become one thing even though the text remains silent. My approach to text that I actually set is different. But the majority of pieces that I write which involve text are instrumental only, with no audible singing or speaking taking place. To try and be more succinct about it: I'll be composing, I enter a certain emotional or psychological space, and then certain poetical texts come to mind, unbidden.

Coming into contact with Christopher's poetry was a central element of my education. Without question Christopher's poetry helped me to grow up, especially in terms of clarifying my relationship with the written word. It provided me a bridge to a greater sense of what it was I wanted to say musically. An odd calmness came over me that autumn of 2001, in Berlin, which of course was a time of global chaos. It was a surreal juxtaposition being in the midst of what was for much of the world, broadly speaking, a time of violence and disquieting uncertainty, and of beginning to see a way forward as a composer. The scaffolding for that clarity was Christopher's poetry. I don't know if it would have happened without him, but it happened in that moment and in many ways everything I have written since stems more from Christopher's influence than from any other artist. That relationship with poetry started in earnest then. I had just turned thirty and I set out on this new path for myself. There were difficult decisions to be made, and to some people it seemed as though I'd thrown away a lot of opportunity, but it all felt so right to me.

Hersch composes his poetry-based pieces – and this has remained his *modus operandi* – not in response to poems in their entirety but to fragments taken from them. What the fragment does is invite the mind to make it complete. What will come of it, however, is not the thing as it once was but something brand new. And there is the sense too, such as we get when inside the remains of an abbey open to the skies, that, at least where imagination is concerned, there is nothing more complete than a ruin. We might mentally construct, and try to complete, those arches, but they resist our finest efforts, saying *we are what we are, you would not be here otherwise.* The poet and amateur archaeologist Gustaf Sobin speaks of 'luminous debris', which may be said to describe the whole of his literary enterprise, the construction of a world upon a single fragment. In one passage in which he meditates on a Bronze Age earring of lunar shape, he writes, 'Aren't we always, indeed, witness to artefact,

to the muffled discourse of the inanimate, to the irresonant world of vestige?'

It is a very powerful, evocative, word, *fragment. Fragment* seems to reside at the heart of how I approach poetical text, which is in stark opposition to how I generally approach music. However, for me the reactions I'm having to these moments within a larger poem are as if these fragments are not fragments at all. They constitute an entirety for me, a complete verbal world which draws me into them specifically for their totality. I realise of course I'm working with fragments of a larger whole, the whole as conceived of by the poet, but to me these text fragments have become a *new* whole, misguided as I may be.

When I asked Hersch whether he was recreating the poem in music the answer was an emphatic *no.*

More often than not the poem seems to be expressing in words something similar to what I am already trying to say through pitches, rhythms and silences. As I mentioned before, it becomes a companion and it is right there with me. I really do not feel I'm setting the poem in or to music; I am already composing, or more accurately put, attempting to compose what it is I want to say, but the text fragment seems to mirror in my own mind that thing I wish to express, and often does it far better than I. There are plenty of examples of composers engaging with a poem or a poetical fragment, and then writing something which attempts to set the given poem to sound. I'm not attempting to do that. One of the reasons it took me some twenty years to finally settle on something for the stage, or why I write song cycles so infrequently, is that I need to feel I can give/add something to those texts. The last few years have been something of an exception as a result of my working with the soprano Ah Young Hong [who premiered the sole role in Hersch's *On the Threshold of Winter*]. Working with a singer that I trust so wholly has been a tremendous motivating force for me to do more with the setting of poetry to be sung. For most of my musical life I was convinced the texts I responded to didn't require anything other than their presence on the page, that even if I wanted to engage it was highly unlikely I could have truly added anything to them. In the purely instrumental works companioned with text I often struggle over whether to share the accompanying text fragments with an audience as the relationship between word and music feels much more part of an intimate conversation between myself and poet rather than something for public consumption.

'It's something almost akin to a kinetic process then,' I suggested. 'A phrase jumps up at you, sparks into sound.'

It either sparks into sound or, as is more often the case, the sound sparks the word in the sense that I'm writing music and then the words appear in my mind. These words are already somewhere in the recesses of my memory. All of a sudden what I'm writing triggers the memory of a poem or, as is more often the case, the fragment of a poem, that inhabits a similar psychological or emotional space.

'There is a lovely line Christopher quotes from Wolfram von Eschenbach's *Parzival*, "It must happen unknowingly." Only then is one fit to inherit the Grail. It *is* involuntary. I am not poring over a text, looking for something specific. I like to read and I search for like-minded poets because it simply makes me feel less lonely in the world. For me the barrier between words and music is very porous. When I consider those two worlds in my imagination, the part that loves words is constantly in dialogue with the musical part of me.

And where does the music come from? Was it akin to the idea of Michelangelo revealing the sculpture already buried in the stone? There is a letter Giacometti wrote to Pierre Matisse in which he describes whittling away at a sculpture until it disintegrates in front of his eyes, which for me has always been a fine expression of artistic terror.

The question is what to do with all that havoc. I attempt to give it voice simply to stay sane. A lot of these impulses are chaotic. Making music is for me the primary way to quiet things within. You attempt to put these demons into sound and silence ... the stakes are high ... high not in how other people will respond, that's not part of it, but high with respect to getting through life. Life provides plenty of challenges. In an idealised world I prefer to deal with musical challenges rather than with those unavoidable ones in the external world. That world, the outside world, is far more terrifying.

   Another thing that astonished me, though perhaps it ought not to have, is that throughout the four-year period of composition Hersch didn't perform a single movement of the fifty that make up *The Vanishing Pavilions*. As one who constantly needs to see how what I write appears on the page, the question I wanted to put to him was not so much *how* he managed to compose in silence but, rather, a simple *why*.

I was convinced that if I'd worked at the piano then no matter what I did my fingers would start to dictate what I was composing. In order to write the best piece I was capable of for the piano, I knew I needed to avoid the instrument itself. I knew that if I sat at the piano I ran the risk of writing only within the limits of my own ability to *play* the instrument rather than *write* for it. I needed to reside within my ear and not in the musculature of my back, arms, wrists and fingers. I needed as much discipline as possible. Ultimately, playing through the work while I was writing it would have been a distraction. It would have simply caused anxiety regarding the upcoming performance of it, and how I would go about physically learning it. I think the piece is better for it having been done solely in my mind. Splitting the process between composing and physically learning it was the right one for me.

'And so how would you summarise your relationship to poetry?'

What the poets I love have accomplished with their poetry is what I am after in my own work. It is a never-ending journey. There is always this struggle to get rid of what is not necessary. I think part of my attraction to words is that somehow I feel I'm able to see that which is necessary more clearly in poetry. It is a struggle. I would like to get

to the bones of my own work. I want things distilled, though I'm not against ornament. It is very much a work-in-progress.

'*Spare* is the word, is it not?' I asked. Hersch paused for a moment.

But 'spare' is a tricky word too. *Spare* is like *fragment*. It is easily misinterpreted. It conjures up the idea of *less* in an absolute sense. That's not necessarily what I'm after. I just want *all that needs to be and nothing else*. I doubt I'll ever be able to achieve that.

M. H. in Cairns studio, 2014 © Sam Oberter

   Michael Hersch is very much his own man, not given to any musical fashion or movement, and when I asked him about influences I was astonished that he listed not a single twentieth-century composer citing instead Josquin des Prez, Carlo Gesualdo, William Byrd, Orlando Gibbons and, to my surprise, Mahler. Expressionism, although he is reluctant to say it, is at the core of his music. The meaning of the word is wide open, however: it applies to every artist he responds to and so as a term he feels it is not terribly useful. The fact that an artist lived five hundred years ago means nothing to him, not when he feels he sees the world through the same eyes. And yet he distrusts the idea of timelessness.

   I think it's fair to say that Hersch's music divides audiences – often, as with his recent *a tower in air* for soprano and horn (2016), right down the middle. This is no bad thing given that new music has hardly got an audience to divide, those who attend to it being, for the most part, already partisan in their sympathies. The ability to delight or outrage is the best thing a composer can have. With respect to Hersch's music I have yet to discover a case of indifference.

   As a composer he will not give what he is not prepared to give. I'll risk the wrath of the furies and say that when he does not bewilder me, which is often enough, I believe him to be one of the most significant composers of our time. Such reservations as I have, and they are few, I have expressed to him and he takes them with good humour. Actually I don't think he much cares. What he does he does because he has to. That's as it should be, although – perhaps just a little optimistically – I'm still waiting for that gavotte.

Three Poems

MARY DURKIN

22–23
Features
Kociejowski
& Hersch
Poems
Durkin

Variations of Beige

We walked
uninvited
into the next village, with the locals exchanged
acute mutual
observation,
and were duly derided by ten-year-old warriors,
waving their French books.
I was struck by
the extraordinary variations of beige
– cream, stone, buff, dun, sand –
it took to make
a desert contrast with flat blue, time-blue, sky,
and the extra shades
– ochre, honey,
sienna, taupe, fawn, drab, khaki – required
for camouflaging
one small village.
And I wondered, on the embarrassed road out,
hot, regretting the
discourtesy
of our intrusion, what picture I'd retain
of the baked village,
the boys, the rat
on the dirt road, recalling the long-legged
Jerboa, who eats
seeds and insects,
nests in fine sand and survives without water,
the lithe African
desert rat, who
Honors the sand by assuming its color;
which we had not done.

To My Friend Taking the Veil

Berlin is beautiful this afternoon.
In Wittenberg Platz trees are silhouetted
against the KaDeWe. The January sky
is low and heavy with tomorrow's snow.
I see at once the scarf folding around you
as you walk to meet me, reserved.
I hear the starlings, crying in dappled branches.
Your raging-tiger face gives way to weariness.

What I have lost from my veiled friends is
irreplaceable. Havens remain dumb
but symbolism is not unproductive.
Whole regiments have been subdued.
Traffic thickens as evening closes the square.
My anger is of no consequence.

Also Amelia *daughter of the above*

There are enough hollow gaping tree trunks with bees and rare beetles
in Abney Park Cemetery
to keep Graham Sutherland and Georgia O'Keeffe going together
in hollow gaping tree trunks
for the many long years it took to age the grave stones, rot the bodies
and weather Sir Isaac Watts on his plinth outside the derelict cruciform chapel
in London yellow-stock with bath-stone facing and octagonal steeple, scaffolded now,
beside the single common lime with nineteen separate trunks,
which has significant regenerative powers.

The Mothers & the Mediterranean

VÉNUS KHOURY-GHATA

translated from the French by Marilyn Hacker

Destroy everything cried the mothers from their high
    balconies
wring the streetlights' necks
make the trees eat dust
dismember the ladder the doll the spider's hammock
The children will play with the Sea
they will learn addition from the corpses piled on the
    sidewalks
subtraction from decapitated trees

*

An eye plucked up from the dust for a pistachio ice
    cream cone for a glass of hibiscus juice –
the merchant on the Corniche trades in everything
    that can be bought and sold

Tanks crossed the Mediterranean
The mothers called the dead and the children to come
    in before the bombardments
wept on their balconies and on the shoulder of the
    rain that rained no longer
green hands plucked the basil that startled at every
    explosion
stuffed the children

*

Only feathered creatures survive said the mothers
who knitted wings for the children
then pushed them off the balcony railings
Fly, my child
my love
light of my eyes
gathered them up from the asphalt with bruised
    hearts
replanted them in the garden at the foot of the sorrel
    that cured colic and calmed fears
Fly into the sun
you'll be a hummingbird when you're ten
a red sparrowhawk feared by the storm when hair
    grows on your palms
fly through air and blood and you'll become a sniper

*

The man who fixed pedestrians in his gun-sights
followed the sun's trajectory
his laughter splattered the blood of the sunset

Planning his night in the evening
his fists cried out on single women's doors
the omelette wolfed down standing
he returned to his roof
begged the rain to dilute him to a timid boy
with a diaphanous mother and a grassy house
his name on a cup hanging over the kitchen sink

*

A relic
the piece of shrapnel rubbed against his jeans
return to the innocence of daisy petals
You love me a little
A lot
Till death...
Tom Thumb's pebbles are the bones unearthed from the
    sand pit
washed with no fuss or tears
since everything was dry
rain and hearts alike

*

The jasmine's white odor makes the fighter kneeling at
    the base of the wall stagger
His machine gun has the soft skin of women with milky
    breasts
His thickened blood cries out at his legs' intersection
The red hole in the forehead of the old woman looking
    for her cat makes him fall down laughing
She got what she deserved
cats don't go to war
Cats and old people indoors
killers outdoors
The country belongs to them

*

Napping in the shadow of his cart
the fruit and vegetable man sleeps with his face against
    the ground
The bombardments startle his cherries but leave him
    like marble
When the war is over he'll have his own cherry tree
a wife just for himself, and children fresh as magnolia
    petals
white as a communion wafer

*

After death, there is nothing
fog on fog
and snow on snow
time in circles
cried a cadaver
But no one believed him
The streetlights panicked to see him walking
The palm trees' hair turned white all at once
A train lay down on the tracks
The old woman who liked to see people die declared
    him an impostor and
the market gardener whose orchard he crossed hung
    himself from a tomato plant

A time to work the earth and a time to rest in it
    declared the market gardener
cucumbers plump as babies' fingers
green peas round as dimples
beans gleaming like earrings
The recipes the mothers exchange made the bomb
    shelter's walls water

*

The widow who feeds her dead man loukoums and
    ginger speaks to him in the stopped clock
Take me with you wherever you are
skylight of my eyes
grass of my heart
padlock of my house
Say those words again that ripped the mattress and
    made the pillow fly away
words of crystal and smoke
the clock is no telltale and the sniper on the roof
    thinks you've gone to America

*

Shaking out a sheet over the window railing chased
    away the sniper and the sun
tapping on the cat's bowl made him feel full
The widow on the floor above the floors walked on her
    tears to cool her burned feet
her footprint a five-leafed clover
A good omen decided the gull standing on his rock
the war will be over before the Mediterranean retreats
    completely

*

The Mediterranean took advantage of the widows'
    slumber to retreat as far as Nicosia
The children who saw it leaving didn't hold it back
the wings on their little shoulders keep them from
    running

Who are you to steal my sunlight? a boy cried out
The sniper, who only fears dogs' barking
took the child apart piece by piece
ranged him in his rucksack, and slept the sleep of the
    just

*

Long life to you, sniper, son of the virgin and the
    carpenter
who can tell the useful from the futile
save us from boredom
save the country from peace
cried a madman from his cell
The madman's words ran in the streets
Their harsh accent rasped skin from the trees
made the waves bristle, ruffled the gull's feathers

*

Minuscule in his gun-sight the sniper's house
his mother a moving point on the threshold
broom raised on her sleeve, the jujube tree stripped
    of its leaves
The odour of méchoui with cumin makes the air
    stagger
lamb chopped parsley shallots
The sniper would trade his kalashnikov for a pinch
    of love and cumin

*

The girl in his gun-sights had walked on his shadow
The explosion tore dress and chest apart
The sniper will follow her funeral from his rooftop
three salvos fired into the air when they lower the coffin
will tear holes in three clouds, and make the air bleed

Tomorrow
the sniper will break his kalashnikov on his knee like a
    straw
Tomorrow
he'll exchange his life for a plate of lentils with cumin
and a glass of arak

*

In the bomb shelter
there is talk of an army of trees ready to invade the
    country
wood-chips fierce with men and bark
they will climb the women and the ladders
plant green children at the hips' intersection
will smoke the beehive till the queen is burnt to ashes
dismember men and drones

*

A time of abstinence, austerity
fingers grown so thin their rings fall off
The widows who stir up the depths of the sea with
    sticks
exhume silent algae and discontented drowned men
the separated husbands are driven back toward the
    open sea
their wrinkled skin pleads against them
and what seemed to be a diamond is salt petrified
    between two eyelashes
There are too many drowned men to count

*

Tired of wringing out their mops in the Mediterranean
the widows sleep against the walls
sleep on their own shoulders
the candle on the threshold chases off the unwanted
    dead man

Meowing of cats and newborns
the mothers are women sold like fish
A heat wave undulates the tarmac
Seen from the balconies, the sea swallows its waves the
    wrong way
its shells an insult to a bellicose land

*

Rainstorms diluted the country
There is another earth under the earth
another sea beneath the sea say the women who
    sweep the sea
treasures worthy of a sultan's palace
the slipper of a drowned concubine
throne of an emperor who set his city on fire
Chinese mandarin's tableware
marshal's baton
dog collar
The Mediterranean gives back what we lent it
The sweepers polish their copper and the Alexandrian
    semaphore with the same mixture of
    ashes and lemon

*

It's snowing on the Mediterranean
The flakes erase the war
The dead no longer tell us their news
the reluctant widows live backwards
daylight breaking into the bomb shelters flows like
    milk
cats lap it up on the cement then wipe their muzzles
    on a stain of sunlight

A cat's corpse in the middle of the road
nauseates the sniper
Kneeling on his shadow
he looks at the absent tree, the nest poised in the air
When the war is over
he will go and live in a nest

*

The mothers' voices calling cats and children cross
    out the clouds
stop the flight of sparrows above the minaret
'Eat, so you'll grow!' they tell the dead children
'Eat, to grow as tall as the ladder'
Luminous bread for the darkened child
Earthy bread for the man who ploughed the sea and
    sowed his rage between two waves
sure of harvesting enough drowned bodies to stock up
    for the winter

*

It's snowing in the cannon's mouths and in the chick-
    en coops
Tossed snow can be eaten raw
The muezzin's call turns into stalactites
Your toes go mad first, the rest follows

The women's calls are a pile of salt on the jetty
The surf brings in shriveled drowned men and books
    that have doubled in volume
The wind predicted for tomorrow will separate the
    pages
and restore to their fate words that cried out in the
    depths

*

In the church that lost its roof
they burn pebbles in the censer
wash laundry and children in the baptismal font
Tomorrow is Halloween
The killers will fold their evanescent wings to come
    through the gate

The Mediterranean's days are numbered
With its water drained off
it's a heap of carcasses and fish bones
Sailors look for its reflection in the clouds
The sniper sees it in his mother's eyes, who knows by
    his smell that he has killed
'Welcome to the child who replaces the child,' she says
and she dresses him as a girl

*

For the women who grew old in the bomb shelters
a country is built above the country
Houses that turn their backs on the waves that tear
    down the doors
and drag the women clinging to their cries out by their
    hair

Poetry for the Future

Thom Gunn and the Legacy of Poetry

ANDREW LATIMER

HOW CAN A POEM be like a novel? Or perhaps a better question would be, why should a poem be like a novel? These were questions that Thom Gunn posited whilst writing his seventeen-part mini-epic, *Misanthropos*. The poem, in Gunn's own words, is:

the account of a man on his own. It is divided into four parts. In the first, he has escaped out of battle into a distant part of the world; on his journey he sees nobody, and concludes that he is the only human being left alive on earth.[1]

You would be forgiven for thinking this the blurb for a sci-fi novel, in the manner of Arthur C. Clarke's *Against the Fall of Night*. *Misanthropos*'s pre-publication names ('The Last Man', 'The Book for the Last Survivor', 'For the Survivor') would only support this preconception. Yet, with its highly formal style and its measured appearance – fourteen out of seventeen sections fit perfectly onto one page – there is no mistaking it for anything but a poem. In fact, Gunn's poem seems obsessively concerned with poetry's formality. In the second part of *Misanthropos*, Gunn plays a clever trick of verse, utilising the highly artificial Renaissance echo-poem to depict his protagonist's first encounter with a post-apocalyptic human:

At last my shout is answered! Are you near,
Man whom I cannot see but can hear?

                               Here.

(Misanthropos II)

Creeping in from the right-hand margin, a space not often occupied by poetry, comes the soft sound of another voice. Or, given the Renaissance form of this section, is it merely the protagonist's own voice echoed back to him? There are six questions, and six responses. Each response, as in the first quoted above, subtly distorts the question in order to form an answer. The trick is visually apparent, but not, as the protagonist receives it, aurally apparent. Simultaneously acknowledging the otherness of his echo as well its sameness, he decides the best emotion for survival is misanthropy, asking:

Is there no feeling, then, that I can trust,
In spite of what we have discussed?

                             Disgust.

(M. II)

---

1 'Poetry for the Future', University of Maryland: http://www.lib.umd.edu/litmss/thomgunn/exhibition.html.

Writing in the unpublished essay 'Poetry for the Future', Gunn states that his 'hope for poetry is that it can once again become a major genre'. At the time Gunn wrote this, Larkin and Davie had been fast rolling down the shutters of poetry, selling off their inheritance for the sake of modesty and irony. But Gunn, under the tutelage of Yvor Winters at Stanford, believed, or wanted to believe, that poetry could indeed become again a form of central discourse within society. It could be 'pure', as Davie would have it, as well as ironic, as Larkin would, whilst taking an experience of modern life and forming a complete statement about that experience. This is what Gunn admired in the novelists of the early twentieth century. From reading the complete works of 'Mann, or Proust, or Conrad, Camus, or Lawrence, or even to take the living William Golding', Gunn could find a 'complete attitude to experience worked out in detail, qualified, supported, given an imaginative realisation'.

Gunn's criteria sound as if these novelists were writing undergraduate essays, where their creativity must be 'worked out in detail', 'qualified' and 'supported'. The claim, nonetheless, is sincere. It was criteria such as these that he saw missing not only from his contemporaries, but from the four major poets of the previous generation: Pound, Eliot, Stevens and Yeats. 'The great modern poets', writes Gunn, 'certainly have as an intense a preoccupation with particulars as any of the novelists' but as they do not 'support' or 'qualify' their experience they do not 'seem to learn from them (to derive from them any body of ideas) that one can take seriously'. The problem, as Gunn saw it, was that they wrote acute, experiential poetry and then fell back on dogma to justify it – Gunn says Pound's ideas seemed rather more like 'prejudice than thought'; Eliot too quickly turned 'psychological-moral' into 'religious-moral'; Yeats was 'extraordinarily reactionary'; and Stevens took 'refuge in a kind of church' called 'Imagination'.

The point is, ultimately, that poetry had lost ground to the novel. In its preoccupation with form, poetry (especially in the case of poets like Pound) had lost its grip on reality. It is an old story by now, one told in every textbook or companion to almost every art form in modernity, of how one art form lost out to another and as such has become fossilised, and minor. Yet of all the art forms, without exaggerating, poetry seems to have undergone the most severe form of diminution, and to have done so entirely at its own behest. Think of all the big poems of the last century, ones that openly address themselves to their society and are long enough to do so. Think of the epics, primarily, of the first half of the twentieth century, such as *The Waste Land*, *The Cantos*, *Paterson*, *Notes Towards a Supreme Fiction*. Although two of those poems sprawl into the second half, they are all largely products of a poetic experiment begun in the first half of the century, generally agreed to be called modernism. As different as they all are, none of them makes a clear case, one that is 'worked out in detail' in Gunn's words, as to why poetry is immediately relevant to its society. Eliot's epic struck at a time when his nervous system was attuned to that of his contemporaries. But the long heritage of squabbling that is *The Waste Land*'s critical history goes to show that Eliot's sense of experience was anything but 'qualified' or 'worked out in detail'. Neither was it supposed to be. Pound expresses the dilemma: 'Artists are the antennae of the race but the bullet-headed many will never learn to trust their great artists'. But when those 'Artists' write verse like, 'OB PECUNIAE SCARCITATEM / borrowing, rigging exchanges, / licit consumption impeded', either the transmitter is broken, or there must be something wrong with the antenna.

Gunn's misgiving about these modernist epics was due to their self-imposed marginalisation. 'They make a leap into abstraction', he argues 'that acts as a denial [...] a leap which none of us want to follow'. Yvor Winters, a neo-classical convert from modernism, traced this 'leap into abstraction' to modernism's experimentation, writing:

Many experimental poets, by limiting themselves to abnormal convention, limit themselves in range or approach: that is, become primitives or decadents of necessity; and they lack the energy or ability to break free of the elaborate and mechanical habits which they have, in perfecting, imposed upon themselves.

What Winters and Gunn are getting at here is the nature of self-imprisonment that goes with the long poem of the twentieth century. Like an academic article, the idea must be narrow and original enough to be pursued in some genuine detail, but in doing so it runs the risk of becoming too obscure. So, whilst Pound may have 'invented' several new methods and mechanisms for writing and thinking about poetry – the *imagiste*, the Vorticist, the Ideogrammatic, the Historical – Gunn's point is that there are few people who are interested enough to go and sniff them out. These poets may have perfected the 'direct treatment of the "thing"', but the general readership no longer knows what the original 'thing' was. Or, to use Pound's analogy of the artist as antenna, what happens when analogue is replaced by digital and societies no longer use their antennae?

This, I would argue, is the complicated and diffuse context behind a poem like Gunn's *Misanthropos*. It is a study of how a poem can be like a novel, particularly a novel in the vein of Thomas Mann, Sartre, and Camus – and a link might be made between *The Outsider* and Gunn's initial title for the poem, 'For the Survivor'. Gunn's understanding of the novel form, in 'Poetry for the Future', largely extends to existentialist literature, as is manifest by the phrase 'complete attitude to experience'. The novel, as a long form of fiction, offers its author certain liberties that the lyric verse withholds. In a lecture given in 1981, Gunn quotes Keats by saying that 'A long poem would be something to turn around

in.' The poets of the fifties in Britain, as part of The Movement, insisted on the short lyric as the most appropriate form for the poetry of their time. Gunn was associated with The Movement, and his first collection, *Fighting Terms*, evinced much of Larkin and Davie's aesthetics. Yet after two months in a hospital bed reading *The Magic Mountain* while he recovered from hepatitis, Gunn had an idea that would be set on a mountain of his own, and as a poem it would be long enough 'to turn around in'. *Misanthropos*, as it was to become, was a chance for Gunn to form his 'complete attitude to experience worked out in detail, qualified' and 'supported' by the opportunity to stretch out in a longer form.

In the same lecture of 1981, Gunn talks about his initial plan for the form of his long poem. He says 'I wasn't up to doing it all in one form [...] I don't know whether this is the fault of the twentieth century, or it is the fault of me'. Here, as he attempts to write the poetry of the future, we are reminded of the poetry of the past – of Gunn's immediate past. The twentieth century is haunted by that leviathan of Frankenstein-form, the modernist epic. These long, polystylistic poems took the form they did partly because of the restrictions set upon them by their authors. Eliot argued that poetry should demonstrate

the feeling for syllable and rhythm, penetrating far below the conscious levels of thought and feeling, invigorating every word; sinking to the most primitive and forgotten, returning to the origin and bringing something back, seeking the beginning and the end.

If this level of interaction of form with content was demanded at all points through a poem, especially a long poem, the form must change to keep in close contact with the content. In order for Eliot's poem to stay close to the wasteland it depicts, to have 'thought and feeling' in line with 'syllable and rhythm' the poet must chop and shift as his material does. In other words, the poem, not just the poet, must constantly seek to 'make it new'. This is a standard that modernism has set for poetry, and for most, if not all, of the arts. It is perhaps its greatest legacy. Yet it has undoubtedly complicated the nature of writing the long poem, as Gunn suggests. So, avoiding the 'imitative form' of the modernists, he seeks to set out his poem in seventeen small, page-length sections utilising forms borrowed from the Renaissance poets, and later poets such as Andrew Marvell. By doing so, Gunn avoids the level of fragmentation that epitomises *The Cantos*, yet he does not avoid fragmentation altogether. *Misanthropos* is not one sustained piece. It changes, evolves, goes back when it should be going forward – but that is to be expected from a poem which is 'a place to turn around in'.

Gunn's protagonist accepts misanthropy as the best philosophy for his time, only to reject it in favour of a different kind of fiery emotion, 'A man who burnt from sympathy alone' (*M. VIII*). If he was to remain misanthropic the poem could hardly proceed. There would be no direction, no movement beyond the one man and his eternal present, 'The momentary feeling / Is merely pain, evil's external mark'. Throughout, Gunn associates the present moment with a form of evil. The poem suggests that living without a sense of the past 'worked out in detail' is a moral failing. Gunn cribs his poem: He becomes the misanthropic man, attempting to eliminate even his own consciousness, because it is reminiscent of the human race. But he comes to realise that the attempt to banish itself is only a sophisticated operation of the consciousness, which he must therefore resign himself to accepting as an evolutionary fact he can escape only in madness or death.

To live, as the poem says, like 'the birds, self-contained' (*M.I*) is a violation of humanity. One cannot extricate oneself from the collective past merely because there was evil in it; it does not go away, as the mind cannot cease to think except 'in madness or death'. Gunn writes:

> he must without regret
> Accept the inheritance he did not choose,
> As he accepted drafting for that war
> That was not of his choosing. *(M. IV)*

The post-apocalyptic world of the poem is the state in which Gunn finds poetry at the middle of the twentieth century. There is dogma appended to experimentalism. The botched forms of modernism, to Gunn, go hand-in-hand with the 'botched civilisation' which produced them. The latter led to war and the destruction of its own people, while the former, the poets, retreated into esotericism: Eliot into his religious moralism and Yeats into his 'nostalgia for feudalism'. It is a remarkably misanthropic mind, however, that would make no good of their work. To progress from the Last Man to the First Man of the future as the misanthrope does, the poet must 'accept the inheritance he did not choose' and design whatever form of long poem the twentieth century will allow.

Misanthropos was performed before it was published, as a dramatic reading on the BBC. As part of the broadcaster's normal procedure there was an Audience Research Report, which played the reading to a panel of listeners and then asked them to fill out a questionnaire. The performance, and the poem, were then graded, or given a Reaction Index (which sounds like a bureaucrat-led post-apocalyptic nightmare for poetry). *Misanthropos* received a score of fifty-nine. The previous year's average score for *The Third Programme*, on which the reading appeared, was sixty-three. To put this in context, Eliot's radio talk, 'The Three Voices of Poetry', received a score of seventy-two.

Remarking on hearing *Misanthropos*, one listener lauded it as 'A series of poems of great relevance to the human condition. The writing was polished to perfection.' Despite some other remarks regarding Gunn's handling of rhythm and rhyme, the reaction was largely one of confusion: 'Too much to comprehend in one reading,' 'An irritating mixture of the mystical and mundane,' whilst many worried that the 'very complex meaning was elusive'. I doubt whether many people today would grasp the meaning(s) in one go at listening to it. The wit of the echo-poem is lost on listeners, themselves reduced to the limited

aurality in which the misanthrope finds himself. Writing in his notebook in 1967, the year in which the poem was published as part of the collection *Touch*, Gunn, looking back on the poem, felt that it might have been 'pompous in its conception'.

In that it stretched the form of poetry, taking it into the terrain of the novel, it certainly was ambitious. Pound envisaged his own *Cantos* as a 'bombastic rhetorical epic'. Perhaps it is a product of the epic terrain, or mini-epic, that a certain amount of pretension has to be invested in the experiment in order to gain momentum, and sustain it. In an interview of 1989, Gunn reflected on this:

Being born in 1929, I grew up at a time when all the great Modernists were still alive and they were still flourishing when I was able to read them. Eliot, Pound, Williams, Marianne Moore, Stevens: they went on for quite a considerable time of my life. They mostly died in the sixties, didn't they? It's very difficult to point to any poets of even comparable stature now. I don't think the poets of my generation have really proved to be very good examples to younger poets. Obviously the most famous and most accomplished poet of my generation was Philip Larkin. Larkin, however good he is, is set against rhetoric – rightly perhaps – and set against daring. Daring is just what young poets ought to be making use of when they're trying themselves out.

Interviewer: Do you think that what Larkin encourages is a fear of being pretentious – that it might actually do young poets good to be pretentious?

Gunn: Yes, you've got to go through that. You've got to make your mistakes.

Taking pretentious as the key concept – its root being *pre* + *tendere* (Latin for 'to stretch') we can see that pretence is part of the life of *Misanthropos*. Gunn wanted a long poem, for 'a long poem would be 'something to turn around in', something within which to stretch. In 'Poetry for the Future' he hoped for a type of poetry that could do what the novel had done previously. In doing so, Gunn had pompously stretched his poetic form. But because of this, can it be written off as a pretentious mistake?

Critical history might suggest as much. The poem has largely disappeared from the critical radar; it is rarely anthologised and was not included in the 2009 Farrar, Strauss and Giroux *Selected Poems of Thom Gunn*. Yet, with its compressed lyric veneer and novel content, the ambitions of *Misanthropos* cannot be completely consigned to history. Rather, the reception of the poem – its below-average 'Reaction Index score' and lack of critical attention – echo the poem's own distrust of the present moment, the fear of 'Hardening in the single present' (*M. VI*). Instead, its epic pretentions and novelistic bombast position it as a poem for the future, preferring the 'Immeasurable, / The dust yet to be shared.' (*M. XVII*)

From the Journals of R. F. Langley

THE POET R. F. LANGLEY (1938–2011) was also, privately, a prolific prose writer. Extracts from his journals, which he began in 1969, first appeared in *PN Review* in 2002. The notes to Langley's *Complete Poems*, edited by Jeremy Noel-Tod, cite a number of unpublished journal entries that directly informed the writing of his verse.

---

14 May 2000, Minsmere Beach, Suffolk

At the top of the shingle the low bank is undercut, draped by dead marram, stuffed with packed flints. But it has a narrow gutter, along its base, of clear sand, maybe where the last high waves tickled out the flints so they fell away. The sand is pocked with small holes. I take a length of marram and poke into one. Half an inch above it a fan of black spider's legs suddenly protrudes from the sand. I poke below these and force a fine arctosa perita out into the open so it runs very briefly, then freezes. Perfect match. The glassy sand grains, in size and colours, match its mottlings, cinnamon, ginger, black, orange. It moves only its chelicerae, a little. After a long time it goes to another hole, under a pebble, pulls itself in, backs out, waits some more. Eventually it heaves itself out of sight under the sand where there seemed to be no hole... the remnants of its old tunnel, possibly. The surface shrugs as it pushes deeper. A dead female minotaur beetle rolled on her back close by, carapace horns short and unobtrusive, dead eyes a stony flesh colour, deader than the glittering silica around her. Stiff fan feet, brittle, grooved black elytra, wedge-shaped head, underslung. Look up and out into the undaunted light. A heat haze hides South-wold, Sizewell. A thin pencil of dark haze parallels the horizon and, below the horizon, level strips of silver stripe the far sea, so sea and sky blend as a ladder of alternating, similarly paired, lines. Pairs of people walk with dogs, who fetch sticks out of the placid foam. Sandmartins chitter. Terns squeak. The spider moves its jaws. Two grains of sand tremble brilliantly, somehow hooked up in the hairiness on the dead beetle. Up here all the flints are bone dry and clanking.

Eight Poems

MILES BURROWS

The Flight from Meaning

I like difficult poets who tease you, difficult girls
Pulling their hair over their faces and running away.
Though this could get tiresome.
Soon it will be time to cycle through the rain to yoga.
I wish I was mysterious.
All I wanted was to be opaque and cryptic.
And later perhaps arcane.
Who wants a Delphic oracle who says what she means?
I left Church as they prayed in English.
And went to Roman mass till I learnt Latin
And had to go to the next street, where mass was in Polish.
When I began to understand a few words of that language
I left for a guru who gave me a meaningless sound.
When that suggested a wave on a tropical beach
I had to leave and go to yoga classes.
Everything is fine now. I can't understand a word.

The Second Affair

Mutus thought that embarking on a second affair
(although 'embarkation' was hardly the word, suggesting
a flurry of cabin trunks, tides, and gangplanks,
and calling to mind, as many things did,
his parents' picture of *A Voyage to Cythera*)
would be like having a second slice of cake
or learning a new language, or going on
to some kind of higher education, as if
proceeding from algebra to trigonometry,
or from Base Camp to the North Face.
No disrespect to algebra, it could even be a logical step.
Or taking out a new book from Boots lending library
so that he could walk slowly along the crest of the road
avoiding the camber on either side
his head buried in the text of a new plot
ignoring all the traffic, and with the bookmark
from the Boots lending library swinging slowly as a pendulum
as he walked.

The Eye Test

I don't want to see too much.
I would like to see Gisela in the half-light by the fence
Close up smelling of creosote
Feeling her scratch my palm in the moonlight
If there was moonlight.
Just a rough image would be quite enough.
I'm not asking for detail or long distance.
Otherwise I can just smell creosote.
I don't want to see Nurse Creeley.
I don't want to see Dr Fonsecca unless he's fallen into a pond.
I can see people clearly but have no idea who they are.
I don't want suddenly to see Caitlin's husband close up
I'd rather see him slightly further away.
As we went along in the steamy heat the head man bent over twigs

Junk Mail

Despite your long silence I write again.
I appreciate that you are dead, but even so
You could light a candle in that other room
And I would come to you singing like Jonas Kaufmann
Demonstrating a controlled diminuendo
On a high E natural. If we were spirits
I wouldn't have to wash. And that intimate sigh
Into the ear that wakes me at midnight,
Is it really from the orthopaedic mattress
Or do they have ventriloquists?
It is possible to fall in love with a woman.
There are people who have fallen in love with a postage
    stamp.
Fortunes have been left to cats
Who never spoke a word and never will.

At Nam Yao

I was reading *Poetry of the Committed Individual*.
The girl at the bar was reading *Structural Anthropology*
    upside down.
The man at the table was reading *Confident Salesmanship*.
I was dreaming I was A. E. Hemingway.
But who was A. E. Hemingway?
That can't be right, even in a dream.
Above the Buddha, a garland of browning jasmine.
You are my horse, my Tang horse.
She leads you by the nose.
Et branle, branle, branle charlotte
Don't give me flowers. I thought it was sad, those young
    girls.
You can tell he is going to kill himself.
You can feel it in the first paragraph.
The rhythm, the repetitions, the dust on the roads.

The Wasp-Orchid

Timing in love: what a theme for the novelist!
The wasp-orchid looks pretty nondescript
but smells like a virgin wasp just out of the bath
(and, this is the point, is always *on time*).

Now the actual teenage virgin wasp is in no hurry to get out of the bath.
ENTER The Young Male Wasp. Beside himself with desire
he plunges blindly into the aroma of the orchid
(which happens to be standing close by in a state of readiness).
He emerges covered in pollen and the indelible illusions of romance.

3 weeks later the real virgin, having overslept,
finds her body odour all over the bathroom,
and the young male turns stupefied eyes towards her
like a novel-reader at the tennis club
who hardly sees the girls on court, being still half stunned
by his life-changing brush with Mme Chauchat.

Hawk Moulting

The poets are out watching hawks again.
They can't get enough of it.
They crick their necks craning upwards
And spin round and get dizzy and fall over.
They are ringing shearwaters on the Isle of Uist in the dark.
What is it about poultry?
A necessary apprenticeship or preliminary fieldwork
That will allow them to proceed to poetry itself.
Their mentors are old crofters speaking Gaelic.
What are they going to do next?
Work in a bird hospital
Mending the wings, the flight feathers all with their peculiar names
They join emergency teams with trolleys scooting along wards
Filled with hoopoes, bitterns, behind curtains
Whooping and crying, some hysterical,
Others with genuine fortitude.

The Old Masters

And just as Goya followed Caravaggio
Or the other way round
So it seemed Mr Robins (Bilge) shared obscure affinities
Of facial expression with Mr Simms (French):
A shaft of sunlight bursting from a grimace
Suggesting memory of melancholic woodland
That was echoed by housemasters' wives in watercolours
Of copses and woods giving scope to intimate shades of umber, dun and russet
And bravura autumnal foliage in danger of toppling over
In old aquariums set on top of boudoir grand pianos,
A *stimmung* reflected even in buns prepared for Thursday evenings
(Cement-like primeval blobs of cornflakes and cocoa)
That old boys would later search for in vain
In the teashops of Budapest
And the bazaars of Transcaucasia.

Mad John's Walk

JOHN GALLAS

ONE HUNDRED AND SEVENTY-FIVE years ago, John Clare, residing at Matthew Allen's High Beach Private Asylum in Epping Forest, decided to go home. 'Felt very melancholy', he wrote, two days before. 'Fell in with some gypsies, one of whom offered to assist in my escape from the madhouse'. Two days later, he was off.

His route, via the Great North Road, was around eighty miles. I thought this doable. First I Googled walking directions from each place he had remembered to the next. Then I bought a pair of Skechers, with Memory Foam feet. I took a spare T-shirt, a spare pair of socks, a rollable raincoat, a hat, the Penguin Clare, a notebook and pen, and my iPod Fitness app, to measure each damned step along the way. John C had old boots, and nothing else. I also had a bank account.

His own account is unfailingly practical: the state of his feet and his boots, the direction he was going, the people he met, and the search for food and a place to sleep were all that concerned him. There is little creative in a desperate pedestrian. And so it proved. The place of his homes, Helpston and Northborough, I know and love. If madness was missing, I felt still that I held his hand all the way, but that we did not talk about Life. Sometimes, that is Poetry.

Day 1 by the app: 48,477 steps, 7 hours & 20 minutes, 26.88 miles. High Beach Asylum to the Baker Arms at Bayford. The wall of Matthew Allen's Asylum, now a private home, has a blue plaque: *John Clare the Famous Poet lived here 1837–1841*. It was exactly 12:00, and my first Clare-town was Enfield. He missed his way early, and so did I: 'till I passed the

"Labour-in-vain" public house, where a person who came out of the door told me the way' (JC); till I asked three youths wheeling a great black pram with silver fittings, ponderous as a coffin, down South Ordnance Road (JG). There were several Enfields: a Chase, a Town, a Highway, an Island Village, a Lock and a Wash. I asked for the Town. In half an hour I was in Silver Street, putting three pages of Google directions in my bag and taking out the next.

To Stevenage. My Google map informed me this would take seven hours and twenty-nine minutes. It was already three o'clock. For JC, this part of the journey was either too easy, or not worthy of memory: 'Steering ahead, meeting no enemy and fearing none, I reached Stevenage', via the Great York Road. This torrent of cars, unending and unfriendly, is denied the walker now. The famous, straight road that JC knew would take him nearly home, once leafy and deserted, was now a roaring speedway. I am sure the absence of memory along these twenty miles was prompted by the absence of his greatest care: that he was going the wrong way. He was set for all. I was lost within a mile.

I stopped at a Turkish garage, where four large men in white shirts held their smartphones at various angles, and directed me back to the Civic Centre in Silver Street. I passed through a mileage of Garden Centres, padding like a Hobbit in the land of Men, past giant fibreglass strawberries with cafés inside, towering kangaroos, bunnies and immense, high fences draped with rampant climbers, enormously vigorous. I then passed a house called Claregate.

The sky was darkling. I asked three women, orange in the sunset, if there was anywhere nearby to stay. They told me there was somewhere that would 'make yer eyes water'; but that down Carbone Hill, and through Newgate Street, there was, also, on the right, the Baker Arms, at Bayford, which did rooms.

Two children behind the bar gave me my keys. The room was vast, and had a bath. I stood at the sash window, which I threw wide open, and looked into the quiet darkness of the village street. Unfortunately, I had forgotten to find its name. I think I was in Hertfordshire.

Day 2 by the app: 66,706 steps, 9 hours & 44 minutes, 34.80 miles. The Baker Arms to the Rose & Crown at Baldock. I strod out early. But quite the wrong way. The street that passed in front of my window was Ashdene Road, which I began the day by searching for two miles away. The frustration and anger visited on a pedestrian by going out of his way is crushing; with John C, it was an obsession. At Stevenage (his first night) he 'lay down with my head towards the north, to show myself the steering point in the morning'.

But Nature is a balm. The bright, sunny morning, leading me by dug stubble-fields and whispering greeneries, through Broad Green to St Mary's Lane, quickly restored me to everything. At a farm gate, I decided to open, in the random manner of a bibliomantic, my Penguin Clare. *I see the sky / Smile on the meanest spot / Giving to all that creep or walk or flye / A calm and cordial lot.*

At Hertford I picked an acorn from a tree and put it in my pack. At Datchworth I drank two bottles of water. At Stevenage I hurried through. Leaving the town I saw, on a hot, wide pavement, a small orange lying in my way. I looked at it. What, I asked myself, would John Clare do? Naturally, I ate it. At Back Lane high trees turned the way into a narrow and wet darkness redolent of dew and liquid foliage. Google told me I was about to enter Damask Green Road. I thought it would be laced with emerald lawns and bushes, breathing a green intoxication from fields made of bolts of cloth laid on the land. Then I got lost. It remains a fair thought sewn upon a landscape. In fact, it contained the Cricketers Arms, where I asked the way to Clothall Road.

Here, two people involved with a concrete-mixer told me that only Baldock could possibly accommodate me. I hurried down the main road into town, facing the terrible onslaught of rush hour. I leapt from tussock to weed on the roadside as cars driven with furious intent lifted my bag off my back each second in their slipstream. I longed for 1841.

It was Baldock Rock weekend. I took a room at the Rose & Crown; small, shabby, and directly above the main door and the street. 'I hope', said the landlady, 'you're not thinking of getting any sleep.' But even the Heavy Metal Holiday below could not keep me awake.

Day 3 by the app: 60,664 steps, 8 hours & 52 minutes, 32.06 miles. The Rose & Crown at Baldock to St Neots. 'I left my lodging by the way I got in, and thanked God for His kindness in procuring it. For anything in a famine is better than nothing, and any place that giveth the weary rest is a blessing.'

After two false starts I was determined to do right this morning. It was drizzling softly. I immediately asked a man with a dog about the way to Claybush Road. His directions were impeccable. I strod on, while the rain thinned in a glitter of air, along a beautiful, waving road, to Ashwell. Here, a child asked me, 'Why are you walking?' If he had had a shilling, John Clare would surely have ridden. To do this journey free of care was to do it for John C, this time without pain. Soon, however, I told myself, I would eat grass, as he did, just to see.

At the junction of Cambridge Road, I was seized by the fancy that I was being followed by a very tall and thin cow. I hardly dared turn around. I knew there was not a real cow behind me, but I could hear the vision, which was alarming. As I continued not to look, its features fell into more and more detail; flat, small ears, an elongated snout, large, mournful green eyes, sunken shoulders, and legs long as stilts. Whatever it was, it was not The Muse.

I reached Sutton, where churchfolk with armfuls of flowers directed me onto a public footpath through Pegnut Woods. It was wet and beautiful, with little bridges over twiddling streams, grass steaming in the sun, and jewelled insects zooming strangely high in the trees.

In Potton, John C called at a house to ask for a light for his pipe. I sat on a bench and ate an apple, and drank a quantity of chocolate milk.

After another brief shower of rain, I strod on. By now, John C's legs were 'knocked up', and he was 'hopping with a crippled foot; for the gravel had got into my old shoes, one of which had now nearly lost the sole'. I bounced out of town in my Skechers.

From Potton to St Neots, I had printed my Google directions backwards. The resulting confusion was beyond all proportion. I asked directions from every person I came across. At Cinques Road I went two miles down a hill to find a signpost that said Potton was very near. I trudged back up: I had walked past a large fingerpost that said 'St Neots 4'.

It was something of a slog. After passing the only thing of interest – a large plantation of elder trees that moaned like widows at a graveside – I entered the annoying suburb of Eynsford, which was very long, in more light drizzle. And then St Neots, where, at the Nags Head, I found a room. Here, John C sat down to rest on a flint heap, where he was told by 'a gypsy girl' to put something in his hat to keep the crown up, or he would be noticed.

Back in my room at the Nags Head, and quite unnoticed, I took another pop at bibliomancy, with my Penguin. *Youth has no fear of ill by no cloudy days annoyed / But the old man's all hath fled and his hopes have met their doom.*

I slept the sleep of the Just.

Day 4 by the app: 62,875 steps, 9 hours & 20 minutes, 32.85 miles. St Neots to Stilton. I strod on towards the Great North Road, as directed by Google, where I was forced to take an alternative footpath to its certain death. It was Google's only mistake. This turned into a very Heaven, all the way to Buckden. Late poppies and birdsong wibbled on all sides. The trees, brighter than bright in the sun, gleamed along the edges of amber fields, like living, silver creatures lined up to watch the tractors putter back and forth, ploughing and turning the earth to chocolate. Here, I thought, of all places, I must pause.

I determined to do two things in this little Paradise: to eat grass, and to find a line in my Penguin that made me weep. To John C, grass tasted 'something like bread', and did him good. I had no need of goodness, and it tasted to me like a pale cloud of beanpod. Standing in the sun, I then wept over *That happy sky with here and there / A little cloud that would express / By the slow motions that they wear / They live with peace and quietness / I think so as I see them glide / Thoughts earthly tumults can't destroy / So calm, so soft, so smooth, they ride / I'm sure their errands must be joy...*

Buckden was rather grand, but very noisy. The A1 thundered by, a never-ending river of appal. From here, John C went 'a length of road', and so did I, via Huntingdon Station, and the Stukeleys. I stopped at a garage and ate three jam doughnuts. I then entered the mystery that is Ermine Street.

This was the old Great York Road, running parallel (and very near to) the A1. To walk on it was to be in constant fear of being mown down, though it was quite empty. The rushing of cars and trucks so close, so continuous, made me turn and look behind a hundred times, where there was nothing. The way was hung with apple trees and blackberry bushes that would have delighted John C, who had, by here, resorted to 'chewing tobacco all day, and eat it when I had done'. It was his lowest point, and his feet were bleeding.

I came to the Stilton Cheese, and stayed. Hereabouts, John C laid down on a gravel causeway, and thought he was a goner. When he rose, and took a direction to Peterborough, he was filled with purpose.

Which would be me, tomorrow.

Day 5 by the app: 38,766 steps, 6 hours & 49 minutes, 18.87 miles. Stilton to Northborough, and John Clare's cottage. I strod on down the A15 in splendid style, imagining, stupidly, that the path would penetrate the suburbs and deliver me to the city centre. It did not. I retreated to the cycle and pedestrian network that makes of parts of Peterborough a strange and stranded quietness, where businesses are silently busy amongst trees, and cyclists swish back and forth alone.

Suddenly, I started to limp.

At the city centre, I sat on a bench next to a man with a Pomeranian on a string. The dog stared at me doggedly. I hurried down Lincoln Road, and continued to Walton, where the blister on my right little toe burst in a moment of tiny pain. I passed Walton, and headed for Werrington. Here, while making for The Beehive, John C was accosted by a woman he thought forward, drunk or mad, who had leapt out of a passing cart. It was his second wife, Patty. 'I got in, and was soon at Northborough.'

I passed through a deserted park, and came to Werrington. I did not take the bus. And I was glad, for the last 3.6 miles (Google: one hour and ten minutes) were an English delight. The cycle path to Peakirk was dappled with sunshine through woffling leaves. The lime-green trees, shoulder to shoulder along the way, flickered light at me with delicious calm. I began to feel proud. I entered Foxcovert Lane, which featured a mighty iron railway-crossing bridge, atop which I stood for a few minutes, and looked out over the fields and rooftops that a twenty-first-century John C would have called home. Glinton spire, so beloved of him, rose occasionally at my left.

Peakirk was quiet as a Monday church, and lit with honey sunlight. I went on, over a little bridge, and glimpsed a spire ahead: Northborough, at last. I stopped for a final random Penguin. *The heavens are wrath – the thunder's rattling peal / Rolls like a vast volcano in the sky / Yet nothing starts the apathy I feel / Nor chills with fear eternal destiny ...*

The church spire turned out to be Deeping St James Priory, and straight ahead. I took a left turn and entered Northborough to the sound of lawnmowers. I opened the gate at John Clare's cottage, and went to touch the front wall. A woman came out, and invited me in for tea. I sat in John Clare's chimney-nook and had my photo taken. Then I hobbled down Church Street, past the graves of his children, and sat in the garden of The Pack Horse, drinking Guinness, and waiting for my lift.

Upon their great returns, great travellers find change and sadness, hand in hand with discontent, and the paler versions of their expectations.

'So here I am hopeless at home.' – John Clare, July 1841.

We walk on dreams, and into reality.

Total by the app: 145 miles.

from Lithos

ANTHONY BARNETT

The Way It Is

It is the way it is. The newborn bird dead on the ground and the rooks wanting it.

I want my life over again. No, not that, I want my life to be, over again.

I wanted to open a book I had written to find in it words other than those I had written.

The mistake has been staring staring at me in the face at every opening.

Later, I may try to tell you a story about going into a bookshop.

Everything can be explained with a dream. Once I did not believe that.

I want to say *it doesn't matter*.

It will always be in the writing.

On the Knife Edge

He finished reading the novel and was struck by the thought that he was no more than a moral coward like the character.

Respites in between

What the Dickens

You must understand
it is the artistry
that must be paid for
but not in money
but in, the blood and sweat they would say,
but in life and
My God, what is the matter with them

On the knife edge

A Little Love Dances in the Blood

a little love dances in the blood

each time I hold my head in my hands I can feel it has grown smaller

who can only deal with what they have

Trees, unresonant word, lining the bank

Always, always, this bank

In the event I am stricken.

And by default the water spills, muggy, sultry, close

close, private the private privet gate

not private to the bird, unresonant word

I hardly need to look at every desirable woman as she walks away, turns back or turns her back, knowingly or not

Play

Man
Woman

I'm waiting for this science silence
so scenic

What?
I don't have to

I have no actors to speak of

I am out of the running

I do not count

He pulls a hair from his nostril between index and thumb
He really doesn't care

Dictate

The Syrian – No one took
                any notice
You cannot clean up your own mess

You went into you want not to

Oh the writer as in
   oh the him *indecipherable scribble*

That's nearly the end of the play

Alleviate

   Diminished. He feels diminished by the behaviour
of certain others and by feeling unsure of his own
ground even as he digs his heels in.

   So much of what he feels impelled imperiled
impeded to write about because of what it arouses
and crowds in on him, is not what he wants to write
at all. It seems to him that it disturbs the thing he
is looking for, which had hajib better be written. To
have got involved with those people in the first place.
Fighting over the bones of a late poet.

   These are not battles to be won. Walk walk walk.
Pretend and preface what you are not. If only he didn't
have to listen to this damn language of his.

   I should respond and alleviate his nervousness.

Readership

It seems I have written to reduce my readership not only
because I am a poet but because I am the one of a kind
of poet I am. I certainly did not set out to write out a
readership but if that is how it is it must be for the good.

untitled

At the point at which you are old
At the point at which you are a wild flower
At the point at which you no longer have a book to read
At the point at which your anxiety has many feathers

A Dead Fountain

I think about what they would have been like when they
   were younger.
I think about what they will be like when they are older.

And what you are when you are out of your stupid uni-
   form.

A fountain not working because it has been turned off. A
   dead fountain.

I looked at the impressed seal on the bench in the gar-
   dens, that someone or other approached, to,
   not exactly, arrest, apprehend, accost.

Not so much that I was tired but that my eyes and brow
   were aflame.

I was not against it because, of course, things do change.

My pen and my notebook in and out of my pocket.

I go out the eternal optimist only to be anointed and
   disappointed.

They are fearful of words like you are fearful in the woods.

Four o'clock thoughts.
A maidenhair yellows before her time.

I hardly remember when I had breakfast, at home or out.
   It was the coffee bar.

THE NEXT STATION IS FRIGHTFULL which is a
   name not an adj.

And You Wake Up

And that is how you take things in. I am feeling
subjewish.

Who do you say thank you hymn?

Flicker of the oil lamp so what a to-do.

Getting the words of others out of one's head
the lamp beside one in the evening.

So I had to write these things down. It was not to be
automatically done pretending to be a writer from a
long ago era.

Is it necessary to judge?

It is necessary to drink.

It burns but it does not burn. Kapo.

The Rest of the World

The extraordinary effort
To make what is not,
That it shall be so
Insignificance. Recognisable
Particles

And should they be as
Affected as they are

Lost in the caffè without
A paper
At that she will come

Restore me
To my imagination
Do not imagine that
What happens is always
What happens

Restore me to the clarity
Beside the sea
In the sea that oceanic
To take away the theory
To be
The focus lost
They have their poetry their poverty
To their backs
Their gracious face
A way of visiting the
Rest of the world

How Do You Grow

The advent, the inversion
Of what
Their lack in swimming their
Lack in failing in everything
But fatelessness. Everything
They have absurdly abused
Even that word, holding the pen
Another way
To awake to walk
Escape unraveled
In a fanciful romance
Very touched very troubled

Holding the pen in another way
So many different ways
It must always come back to that
Resolving the classical real

The advent the inversion

No god will come of this

I look into the sea
The sea of escape
How far away these things escape
The sea of escape

The table boards are sticky
Unending

How do you grow into your
Face

Writing away
Manoeuvring, oh stuck
Oh staunched

I am lost without papers
I do not remember
Whatever it was I wrote down
I do. Yes, I do

So much thrown into disarray
To fold to hold firm in the face

Intimidated by the
Wrench of the
Poor but the
Wealth poor in intellect

Whatever it will be said
I cannot grasp
It worryingly

Thin Air

If you vanish into thin air and appear out of thin air

The fragments are a kind of protest, a test
For the reader, if there is a reader

I do not use chemicals
My alcohol intake is rational
Yet I can still re-enact my history

It is my duty O Lord of the Earth
To bring together such fragments
Every great poet is an arrogance
But I am not sufficiently arrogant
For you to understand me

Bound by freed from

These are the mornings my hair stands on end

And, anyway, what is greatness?
History does not know
As you, you poet, you so-called poet, go down in posterity
To sink without trace

Now they will never know what the drafts may have said

The Order of the Alphabet

And to think that yesterday I had dressed in my best
and today I had not bothered

I had not forgotten you whom I can hardly say I lost

I go back as far as you

There we are faint-hearted again

Swimming floating but not in the sea

I shall be difficult if you know what I mean
I shall not be difficult if you do not know what I do not
mean

Who or what shall be master
Because there is one

Of still the politico class
          oh nasty ambition

And cared no less

You cannot be sure of the order of the alphabet

Oh My Black Beauty

Oh my black beauty, sparkling beauty spectacled

Oh, I dare you dear your delicious despicable

Wear not gloves when turning

I too attach the poem to a juniper twig and decorate the
house with gourds, branches of kaki unless you prefer
the word persimmon

Against the curve, the Asian curve of the wood, though
African part barrel, very restful

O that I should pay myself and forget my spectacles for
the hour

The same old stories

And you will place yourself in the place of the rider
As he becomes the

Nothing

Important

This morning I received a disconcerting message at the
same time as it is
Welcomed

Why the pearl, why the temptation

Writing has become all but impossible

Looking up every few minutes to see who might be passing

Oh go away

True, not true, reading has become almost impossible
Indefensible indispensable

I am indeed stumped. Lost without handwriting. Hand-
written. Disturbed.
Time to go out.

Armorial

'Four Muses' & Other Poems

KATHERINE HORREX

Four Muses

What to say to my muse the power plant
who makes auras for the city's night hours
with a sputter of wattage and volts?

What to say to my muse the steelworks,
who sends hot blasts down the standpipe
for fig trees to thrive in?

What to say of the pigments
rolled out in testing chambers
by my latest muse the chemical plant?

What to say when the power plant
hums and clicks and shines
like a fairylit woodwind instrument?

What to say when the belting out
of playground pieces gives way
to the making of girders for steelworks?

What to say when McBrides carpets the Roch
and makes soft, six-foot dams
out of flammable detergent?

How to contain them all
and do justice to their invention of
and disregard for protocol,

how to juggle their sweltering egos
when I walk where figs
leave oily splats on the towpath,

street lamps turn pale in daylight
and latex dries in a bucket slung round
a rubber plant's tapped green trunk?

Grey Natural Light

It breaks through voile curtains
and stains like tannin leaching into a teacup;

(the voile bunches like tissue paper
strewn by an elephant).

Carbon filters into rooms
invisibly, on the back of the world's breath.

Dioxide. It is not unexpected.
Nor is it hindered; almost every car

trails ashes down the roads' long
crawl of grau, grau, grau. Not much

today it seems will grow but we may dig
for graphite, paint elephants in the sky azure.

Iron Trees
After Ai Weiwei

From vendors in Jingdezhen
tree parts were gathered by the dozen,

long staffs chewed by the delicate lanterns,
by wood ears puffed up with poisons.

The trunks had chatter marks from fungi,
ashen nebs the shape of Shanghai,

maps of the studio's neighbourhood,
criss-crossing into the roughwood,

Shields wrought with pulp and wasps' nests
emerged from the foundry casts

to be bolted at quizzical angles,
quaint as a lamplit English shambles

until the ferrites did their work
of weaving through the bark.

Rust, the trees' deepening autumn,
coats each reaching limb with red, red lichen

and lava-coloured sap sets in
to the notches, the striation.

Night looks down at our undead trees,
the governments composed of dynasties.

Goatfell

Only after living in its shadow for a month
can I say that its attraction has worn off,
that I went there once or twice
seeking a river locals mentioned
not long after I arrived,

nose raw with the churchy strangeness
of water underfoot and the valley
closing over like a hand. My boots
were sucked by moss and a slip in the mud
nearly had me kneeling

as if I were a pilgrim at the island's altar.
More like it was the butcher's block
in the craggiest backstory of this particular ayr
and what I'd heard before meant that halfway up,
when the wind ran round a slate grey howff,

it seemed to whisper 'Rose, Rose.' The way a boiler
in an old, old house takes on the voice
of someone who's not there. Now I do not want to go
into that cold mountain dream with feet scrying
for the summit in the screes and murder in the
    fellside's bones.

Edwin Morgan: A Translator's Notebook

1. Morgan on, and in, Translation

JAMES MCGONIGAL

THROUGH CONSTANT EARLY WORK of translation from a dozen languages, Edwin Morgan explored and re-defined what his own poetry might become. He also clarified what translation itself ought to be. Sometimes he would use this experience in lectures, articles or reviews, and he carefully preserved those among his hundreds of files donated to Special Collections in the University of Glasgow Library.[1] The Edwin Morgan Papers also contain unpublished translations in typescript or holograph versions. Although he had no single notebook of translations, preferring to move quickly from pencil drafts to typewritten sheets, his mainly unpublished papers on translation help us reconstitute his creative thinking in relation to the poetry of other cultures. For Morgan, the 1950s now appear as a crucial decade in which the expanding linguistic range of his translations opens a door into the more adventurous and life-affirming poetry he would write in the 1960s.

Over the weekend of 23–26 March 1956, Morgan chaired a symposium on 'Translation', introducing the session with a detailed paper. This was at the Sixth Annual Conference of Non-professorial University Teachers, in the University College of North Staffordshire, Keele. The conference title and venue signal a more hierarchical age, and perhaps prepare us for entry into a seemingly exclusively male world of translators and lecturers, with an occasional 'colonial' reference that would now be differently handled. More interesting, and still quite radical, is Morgan's subject matter, particularly as he strives to balance the claims of poetry and translation in the teaching of literature, and as he shares insights into the process of translation. (Also prescient was his engagement with current developments in Machine Translation, which would influence our world and his own computer poetry – but which demands separate consideration.) His syntax is complex, possibly slightly defensive, as if aware of the challenge presented by his approach, which is clearly written out of an emotional engagement with translation as well as an intellectual one. My editing is signalled in the text. (J. M.)

*

TRANSLATION

Translation presents itself to any investigator as a collection of problems and difficulties, some of them apparently unsurmountable. Yet to the practitioner it presents a different face: something inscrutably appealing, something that quickens the desire to write, to disseminate, to communicate. Between the critical pessimism of the investigator and the sympathetic enthusiasm of the practitioner there has always been a gap, but that gap is narrowing, and it is from a point of view inclusive of both sides that I want to speak. [...]

The chief argument against the translation of poetry is that too many factors are involved and therefore adequate control is impossible. When a man reads a poem in his own language he is the focus of a very complex activity. When he reads, he receives, from the denotative value of the words, a somewhat intelligible impression of statement or argument; this impression is deepened, but also to some extent confused, by a pattern of connotation rising out of the word groups, since in poetry almost every word takes and gives meaning from and to its neighbours; also, a part of the impact may be visual or pictorial, as in Chinese poetry or E. E. Cummings; at the same time he is listening to a kind of music – being swayed by rhythms and pleased (though often obscurely) by sound-effects; he is looking through a window, but the panes are leaded by the grammar and structure of his own language, which therefore form a part of the poetic experience; and lastly we must be clear that this is an event that involves the whole man: if we call it an act of aesthetic contemplation it is also a physiological disturbance, shown not only in the pulses of the brain that can be recorded (if not yet interpreted) by the electroencephalograph but also in the well-attested incipient vocalisations or kinaesthetic movements that take place in the throat – quite apart from any more gross or flesh-creeping reactions personal to each reader. Fortunately, all these things are resolved into a single experience by the reading mind; it is the translator who begins to see them as separate problems. A couple of illustrations of this may be useful.

If we had to translate Shakespeare's 33rd Sonnet, which begins 'Full many a glorious morning have I seen / Flatter the mountain-tops with sovereign eye', we should not imagine that the first line would cause any great difficulty to someone who understood the words. Yet in the Russian version of the Sonnets by Samuel Marshak, the editorial comment points out that the phrase 'glorious morning' could not be directly translated because 'glorious' in English and 'славный' in Russian have quite different backgrounds of association, whether spoken or poetic, and the English application of the word to weather or atmosphere, with the feeling of bright sky and sunshine, could not be brought out by its Russian equivalent which might rather suggest victorious troops and a bloody field. That is the problem of connotation.

The problem of an unfamiliar syntactical structure is raised when we translate Chinese poetry into English. The central question here is how far we should try to reproduce the effects which in the Chinese

1 See *http://special.lib.gla.ac.uk/manuscripts/search/detail_c. cfm?ID=5*. The talk on 'Translation' is in MS Morgan E/2/1.

poem are clearly inseparable from the structure of the Chinese language. I call this the central question, and yet it has not been solved by even the most generally approved translator, Arthur Waley. A line of Chinese poetry will usually have a regular number of syllables, say 4 or 5 or 7, and usually each syllable will represent a word, and most of these words will be significant words (i.e. not mere grammatical indicators such as English is cluttered with). The question is, must these lines be *expanded* in the attempt to produce an intelligible English version, so that their clearest blocks of syllabic music are lost, and also the characteristic pleasures of their economy of syntax? Hugh Gordon Porteus goes some way towards answering this query when he gives two versions, one literal and the other expanded in the customary fashion, of a poem in the Book of Odes. The poem is called 'The Petition of Baroness Mou', and here are the opening lines, first in the literal translation:

timber gallop timber lash: return console Wei marquis:
lash horse desperately-far: I go to Tsao-waters:
great lord highlands streams: my heart pattern of sorrow:

And here is the final version in 'proper' English:

How would I have whipped round the horses, urged them
    with spurs,
In order to follow and solace the marquis of Wei!
All the long road would have galloped my horses and spurred
Till we came to the waters of Tsao! Great is my lord
but away, over highland and stream:
And the heart contracting in sorrow.

Now the first version may be obscure or at least ambiguous, but the second version has obviously gained clarity at the expense of almost all the structural and formal pleasure of the original. I don't know the solution to this problem, but it should lie in some compromise between Chinese and English idiom, especially by building on such real structural similarities as do in fact exist between the two languages. In this connection it may be pointed out how, on the lowest level, Pidgin English is a recognition of an important fact: that syntax and morphology are not so irreducible, not so peculiar to each language, as we often think. When the New Guinea tribesman looks up at an eclipse of the sun, he cries: 'Kerosene bilong Jesus Christ e bagarap finish!' That may not be English, but it is intelligible, and it even contains what one may call a rude poetry.

These two examples I have given from Russian and Chinese illustrate two poles of the difficulty: the one is the translator's search for the right connotative impact of the individual word, the other is the translator's attitude towards the pervasive structure and logic of the whole language. I have instanced these as among the *separate* problems into which a poem analyses itself when it is examined by a translator, and from a practical point of view translation is a series of related but distinguishable problems, involving continual acts of choice, among many alternatives. In this sense the translator's activity is and must be very conscious and critical: indeed it includes, if properly done, a full literary criticism of the poem, since it has to decide both what meaning the poem represents and what variations of force and value the meaning emits from point to point. But this, in itself so difficult and laborious, will not be enough. The translator must aim at producing a poem, and he will not do this unless he can draw on a very extensive awareness of the resources of his *own* language; without this he is wasting his time. We must be chary of using the word 'creative', but it is the translator's duty to give the *impression* of an act of creation, and this is the most interesting and elusive part of his activity. I think it involves, in some sense of the words, his being a poet; it involves a mysterious switch from the critical to the affirmative, from the humble to the independent, from analysis to synthesis; and it involves a tacit recognition of the importance of random as well as controlled mental searching. I may perhaps describe my own experience in this matter, since I have not seen it described elsewhere.

When I have the poem I want to translate in front of me, I first of all try to sum up its general appearance: its symmetry or ruggedness, length of line, use of rhyme, close or open texture, curious or common vocabulary, and so on. I like this early reading to be, again, impressionistic, since it is important to remain true to these shocks and splashes of impact, representing as they do one's first sudden glimpses of the foreign poet's world, which one is about to enter. For example, long before one *understands* a difficult poem by Eugenio Montale, his world stirs and reveals itself: there is a shimmer, a play of light on water and on crumbling buildings, a face glancing in a mirror, an accordion being played in the twilight... Absorbing this atmosphere is a step in comprehension, and one grasps at this point not only the tone of a particular poem but the signature of the author's style; one begins to sense his 'hand', his way of putting things. At this stage, too, I find most poems yield more *pleasure* than they do at any later moment of understanding, and it is often with great reluctance that I look at them more closely. This, of course, bears out Coleridge's remark that 'when no criticism is pretended to … poetry gives most pleasure when only generally and not perfectly understood'. But then criticism must be pretended to: I treat the poem as an object, degrade it to an intellectual puzzle or code, lay bare the hard core of its meaning with all the external aids of dictionary and grammar, going through it word by word from beginning to end. Once the poem has survived this ordeal, I have at the front of my mind a grid or sequence (I might call it a pattern) of meanings, and somewhere at the back I have a flickering web (which again I might call a pattern) of pictorial, acoustic, and generally atmospheric or sensuous impressions. My job is now to focus the grid of meanings onto the web of impressions; when they coincide, I feel that I can see the poem. This last stage is a combination of range-finding, piano-tuning, and sight-testing; it involves speaking the poem aloud many times, as well as brooding over it in silence. I have now reached the point where translation can begin, and I try to put off translating until this point, although possible words and phrases often suggest themselves right from the start. And something very curious happens here. When I begin to translate, I am searching for an English equivalent, but an equivalent of what? Not, apparently, of the Italian words of Montale, but of *the poem itself*, which has attained some sort of non-verbal interlinguistic existence in my mind. When I used just now the metaphors of the hard grid and the moving web I tried to indicate this existence, but I find it very difficult to describe more closely. I can only assume that the brain has recorded a pattern of impulses which by their nature were only partly verbal in origin, and that in the process of organising the discrete impulses of the poem into an intelligible unit the brain transforms them into its own language, the language of nervous or (as it may be) electrical energy; and the poem that the brain stores, the *deverbalised* Italian poem, is in some way made accessible to the translator who proceeds to *reverbalise* it into English. I have no desire to be mystical, and I hope I am appealing to the experience of others who are accustomed to translate poetry; at any rate, there does seem to me to be a sense in which the poem exists independently of the language of its composition, and I shall return later to this somewhat startling experience in another connection.[2]

[...]

Since in most poetry it is easier to give an impression of the content of the poem than to reproduce its stylistic peculiarities, it is sometimes argued that for all practical purposes a poem may as well be turned into prose. We want to know, it is said, what the foreign poem is *about*; and this we can readily learn from a close and accurate prose account of it. Ironically enough, it is often in the interests of accuracy that this argument for partial translation is maintained. Verse, rhyme, unnatural word order, alliteration are all thought to confuse the issue, and to interpose a veil between the meaning and the ordinary reader.

One recent large-scale effort at translation is instructive in this respect. The Penguin Classics, under the general editorship of E. V. Rieu, are on the whole a most useful and praiseworthy collection, but the editor's principles on this matter of prose or verse are not clear, and there is much to be said against some of his decisions. Sophocles and Dante appear in verse; Homer, Lucretius and Camoens appear in prose. Of these, Homer's *Odyssey*, by the editor himself, comes out the best, and that is because it so obviously tells a story and reads like a novel; here is such a painless poetry that the reader is only occasionally disturbed by its presence. The translator of *The Lusiads*, W. C. Atkinson, lets the cat out of the bag in his Introduction when he says, 'The present translation is believed to be the first into English prose. It aims at rendering a service to the living, not pious tribute to the dead, and is concerned therefore with the substance, not the form, of the original.' This seems to me a rather shocking attitude, since it shows scant respect either for poetry, or for Camoens, or for the common reader about

whom the translator appears so solicitous. On the other hand, we have the jaunty bouncing *terza rima* of Dorothy Sayers's Dante, and the rather earnest ordinariness of E. F. Watling's blank-verse Sophocles. Neither of these translations would reconcile us to believe in the superiority of verse. Still, I feel sure it is verse translations we should strive for, and we shall never improve them, or develop our theory of translation, if we continue to fall back on prose. In many other countries it is considered axiomatic that only verse can represent verse; in Russia especially, where translation is highly developed, excellent poetic versions of foreign poets are continually being produced (often done by leading poets) and sold in larger numbers than the Penguin Homer. One great drawback of course is our lack of anything approaching a *common style* – a way of writing verse that would bridge the gap between an ordinary person's vague idea of poetry and the ideas held by its most advanced practitioners. I suggest, nevertheless, that to attempt serious verse translation, which must be both lucid and yet semantically exciting, will help us in our re-attaining of a common style. The two things go together. If we really believe in the communication of poetry, we shall find this out.

In Old English we have the equivalent of a foreign language. It has a literature, in verse and prose, which we want people to be aware of. This is part of their cultural heritage, and some if it has considerable absolute value. The question is, how useful are translations of that literature, and should they be in verse or prose? To answer this we must begin at the beginning.

There is no doubt that the study of Old English in universities is largely a linguistic study, and in some places (as it was in my own time in Glasgow) what is called a linguistic discipline, the spinal column of the otherwise fleshy and sensuous school of English language and literature. That this should be so is partly inevitable, since students have to learn the language, and it will be at least a year or two before they know it well enough to read and enjoy Old English poetry. Usually they are just reaching this point at the end of their course, and then they go out into the world and never look at Old English poetry again. No one is very happy about this state of affairs, and it has been found increasingly desirable to deal with Old English literature as one would deal with any other literature, on fully appreciative and critical terms. A poem may be a linguistic text, with interesting Northumbrian forms, but it should also be treated as a poem. If this to be practicable, in the two or three years at our disposal, we have to make some use of translations, and, in my opinion, of both verse and prose translations of poetic texts. The one strong argument against this is that students will be too easily satisfied and will never make the effort of ferreting out the heart of the Old English poem for themselves. They will be like those to whom Proust is Scott-Moncrieff, or Rabelais Sir Thomas Urquhart. I admit this danger, but I would urge that it is better to have Scott-Moncrieff and some acquaintance with the French text than to have a deeper knowledge of French grammar and a confused uncritical

---

2 The later connection is with machine translation by computer, and the implications this holds for developing a universal grammar.

skimming acquaintance with *À la recherche du temps perdu* as a work of literature. Naturally, one hopes that in any case students will take a sensible view of translations, and see them as adjuncts rather than as substitutes. One way of encouraging this (although I am aware of the risks it involves) is to include translations in editions of the main Old English texts. I would like to mention the Russian practice in this matter. There is an Old Russian epic poem, слово о полку угореве, 'The Tale of Igor's Raid', which might be called the Russian *Beowulf*. It is a work of great literary power, and it is also a formidably thorny linguistic text. There are several scholarly editions with full apparatus, and this full apparatus almost invariably includes more than one translation – preferably at least three: a close prose version with running parenthetical explanatory notes, a poetic version from some past period (usually by a nineteenth-century Romantic poet), and a contemporary poetic version by a Soviet poet. This may sound something of a Charlotte Russe; but having worked with these editions I think there is a lot to be said for the idea. In Britain, we probably tell our students, 'If you must read a translation at all, stick to a prose version.' This is sound advice up to a point, since they won't be asked to give verse translations in examination answers, and they tend to look on *Beowulf* as a text they will some day have to turn into modern English prose. But if they also have to appreciate *Beowulf* as a poem, and write about it as poetry, then they will be helped if they can compare verse and prose translations with the Old English text. It is the old question of content and form again. Prose for content, verse for form, but who wants form nowadays? A. C. Bradley said, Verse, but even verse will be for content rather than for form. And on my view, if we exert ourselves to produce translations that are both accurate and vigorous, verse will be less apologetically employed, and prose will become the succedaneum. It may seem paradoxical, but verse translation of Old English – and of Middle English too – has hardly begun. It is only in recent years that the mere demand for accuracy has reached a high level; and this still has to be followed by a demand for poetry. Poetry without accuracy is, I think, a declining satisfaction, though a stout fight will no doubt be put up for Ezra Pound's 'Seafarer'. [...]

*

The use of Old English as a reference point ultimately derives from Morgan's long-lived verse translation of *Beowulf* in the 1940s. This was published by Hand & Flower Press in 1952 (after Morgan's unsuccessful attempt to have it considered for Rieu's Penguin Classics) and then by the University of California Press, to be reissued by Carcanet Press in 2002. It still sells. But it seems to be Eugenio Montale who was at the forefront of his mind in 1956, as a translator and also as a young poet in search of an authentic voice of his own. Montale is presented in the lecture as an exemplar of Morgan's own practice, encountering in the process of translation a sort of *Ur*-poem which both the translator and the

original poet (the twin EMs) seemed to share. Such 'co-ownership' was doubtless comforting at a time when his own poetry was proceeding slowly, and when journal editors often accepted his translations for publication but returned original poems with regrets. The list of holograph poems for 1956 reveals that after the conference he worked on translations of Montale to the exclusion of almost all original work.[3] This focus is recorded from May onwards, sometimes leading to several translations over a two-day period. These would form his first full collection of translations, *Poems from Eugenio Montale* (1959), with the Italian text of twenty-one poems printed with facing translation and published by the School of Art, University of Reading. Morgan's Preface to this collection, reprinted in *Collected Translations* [CT: 3–4], suggests he had already discovered a personal sense of identification with Montale (as he would also experience with Vladimir Mayakovsky, Sándor Weöres, Attila József and others), and which he came to see as an important factor in effective translation.

Although the holograph translations are all dated after the Keele seminar in March 1956, Morgan included '35 Poems from Eugenio Montale' in a file of typescript translations and dated these 1955–1960. So his attraction to Montale must have preceded this talk on translation. Some of these versions did not appear in *Poems from Eugenio Montale*, and remain uncollected. Their overall sense of stoical isolation, longing and threat might suggest that Morgan was finding in Montale's hermetic work echoes of his own fraught life as a gay man in Scotland's dour and Calvinistic 1950s. In his work of translation, we might say, he was learning to translate himself. This uncollected translation from *Ossi di Seppia* reveals his determination to reflect both the form and tenor of the original:

CIGOLA LA CARRUCOLA DEL POZZO

A creak is struck from cranking of the well,
The water melts in the light it mounts to.
A trembling of memory in the brimming pail –
On the pure disc lies a laughing image.
I bend my face down, down to vanishing lips:
The past is changed like shadows, it grows frail,
It goes to other arms...

                 Ah, the wheel's rage!
It grinds already to give you back to the pit,
To the blackness, my vision; so far apart we range.

---

3 Available at *http://special.lib.gla.ac.uk/manuscripts/search/results_ca.cfm?ID=1510*

An Encomium for John Fuller at Eighty

ANDREW WYNN OWEN

In years to come, when styles and times have altered,
He'll stand to symbolise so many things.
He'll represent the warmth of Magdalen College,
Oxford's most tranquil, leafy, unobtrusive,
And friendly undergraduate abode;
He'll represent the long-awaited lifeboat
Of regulated wit and sparkling judgement,
The spirit of the eighteenth century;
He'll stand fast as the thoughtful face of England,
Holding the olive branch of contemplation
Above the fray of mercenary distraction.
In years to come, his work will be a beacon,
Uniting all who care for lucid sense,
And, when he's gone, we'll miss him and we'll wonder,
As we now say of Auden, 'How precisely
Did he achieve such playfulness and poise?'
For years to come, I pray he will continue
To flourish. He is sheerest 'floreat'.

At Florio, the Magdalen society
For luring poems out of people's lips,
He sits inscrutably and watches all.
Occasionally, a crease will cross his brow;
Occasionally, an animating smile;
Occasionally, a quizzical expression
That signifies the imminent deployment
Of kind but devastating counter-thought.
Ringmaster, sleuth, intelligencer, he
Co-ordinates the whole shebang with such
Good sense that even supersonic comets
Change course according to his gravity.
His way is difficult and few can follow,
But those who do discover a strange freedom,
The freedom to control the heart and lungs
With words, protean instruments of thought.
So what is Florio, in practice, really?
La Scuola di Fuller, finest school of verse,
Which only asks that students wish to learn
And will not teach but walks with and responds,
Encouragingly or reflectively.

And yet, his output must be centrepiece
In any tribute worthy of the name.
With fairytales and carnivals and puzzles,
Illusions and epistles, he's designed
A world of ploys to raise the public discourse.
His recent work, from reading Dickinson,
Has scanned the calming Wales of sea and sky.
Meanwhile, his scintillant ghazals have opened
The lockboxes of sound that lurk around us.

His masterpiece is due for publication
In January and cannot fail to prove
The fascinating emerald in his crown:
The Bone Flowers is a frolic of a type
Unlaunched in English letters (at least not
With such fastidious handling) since the later
Lord Byron, fusing Ariosto's verve
(That liquid skill, those harlequin digressions)
With Tasso's stern and tragic questing force.
It is, I think, the finest English epic
Since Barrett Browning's wise *Aurora Leigh*,
Inheriting her subtle distillation
Of melody, deliberate design,
Ironic humour, total competence,
And unrepentant mockery of power.
It carries, at its heart, a set of sonnets
Purportedly by Shakespeare, which explore
Age as an older, wiser Shakespeare might
Have hoped to do, if willing to amass
The ripened harvest of his graceful knack.
It is a work to cherish and esteem,
A tale that gives the public what they like
From writers: narrative and nous and stark
Reflections on the brevity of life.
It feels astonishing to say it but,
Seeing him go from strength to strength at present,
I think more striking work is yet to come.

Yes, here he is and we can only wonder:
An advocate of regulated freedom,
Both pragmatist and platonist, determined
His whole life long to up the arts of peace
With that unresting leisure only found
In academics and insomniacs.
I praise him not because he is so bright
And aggravatingly au fait at chess,
But for his generosity, which shines
Through life and work, inviting every reader
To join him in the timeless verbal dance.
Considering his style, I am reminded
About a bit in Arnold I adore:
He says that Byron thrilled us like the thunder;
That Goethe showed us where we hurt; that Wordsworth
Worked to make us feel. Just so, of Fuller,
I'd write: he cleared a space for us to play
And puzzle at the terms of being's riddle.
He picked the lock of life and then devised
A grand piano from the mechanism;
He showed us, with an ectoplasmic lens,
The throng of ghosts that goes wherever we do;

And, more than that, he held his own with Death,
Who grew to see him as an honest rival.
Making us think about mortality,
He sings of Death as no one else has done
Because, in Death, he's met the only mind
Who cannot be diverted or improved,
Whose motivations will not show themselves,
Except as glaring absences of light.
Death says, 'John Fuller, it is up to me
To take you on.' John Fuller laughs, 'But look:
The pigeons in the fountain. Death, my dear,
The figs. The frog. The sunset and the shires.
Do you propose to interrupt all this?
Would you deprive these wonders of description?

Besides, as Hemingway once said to Pound,
One cannot die while writing terza rima.'
And Death, the Great Destroyer, starts to smile
And says, 'I envy you your love of life.
Go then, John Fuller, letting it be known
That you are one of those who made Death smile.'

In 2017, he reaches 80,
And I must say how grateful I remain
To understand the little that I do
Of what has motivated and concerned
This rhythm-fiend and figure out of fable,
This Ferdinand turned friendly Prospero,
The pensive puzzler who conversed with Death.

In Conversation with John Fuller

ALAN HOLLINGHURST

Alan Hollinghursrt: I was noticing some numerical coincidences. The first poems in your first book (*Fairground Music*, 1961) you wrote when you were seventeen in 1954, the year I was born. Then I met you when I was seventeen and became your pupil the following year and began to write under your encouragement. I think it was the time of *Cannibals and Missionaries* (1972). So your work has been a constant part of my adult life...

John Fuller: Golly, you are making me scour my memory.

A. H. I'm going to do a lot of that. You are now publishing, to mark your eightieth birthday, a poem which is a sort of homage to Auden's *Letter to Lord Byron* which he published in 1937 when you were born and he was thirty. So you're publishing yours at an age exactly fifty years greater than that at which Auden published his.

J. F. Yes, *The Bone Flowers.* It's a homage to Byron himself, really, in ottava rima. Auden only managed rhyme royal, one line less. But Alan, I'd no idea you were such a brazen numerologist...

A. H. I don't know what significance there is in these numbers but it made me want to ask you things I have never asked you before. What is your first memory of Auden or your first experience of him?

J. F. I remember reading *The Orators* at school and being so struck by its utter incomprehensibility and busyness that I wanted to imitate it at a time when I'd perhaps only been writing pseudo-Georgian poems.

A. H. At school? When you were at St Paul's?

J. F. I was sixteen in 1953 when I began to write. Yes, *The Orators*, particularly the wonderful prose, so dense and beautiful. In my last year at prep school we had to keep a little book and write down poems in it, things like Noyes's 'Highwayman', 'Overheard on a Salt Marsh', those classic Georgian poems, but also Eliot's 'Preludes'.

A. H. Were you encouraged to learn them by heart and recite them?

J. F. I dare say we were. I am very bad at knowing poems by heart. It is part of being somebody who has always written for the page rather than the ear. The glamour of the page is important and anything else is just, you know, whispers on the wind. There is a more important inner ear that comes into operation when you are reading on the page...

A. H. So from early on you were living in a culture that was encouraging you to think about poems?

J. F. School was rather repressive in some respects. I remember the Surmaster confiscating Joyce's *Ulysses* from a boy who was reading it. Any culture or encouragement of culture came from other sources. Writing poems was suggested by other boys, as was learning Esperanto or the violin.

A. H. Did you have any sort of poetry-writing club at St Paul's?

J. F. No. The first things I wrote with a sense of remembered intention and seriousness were for a school competition with a set subject: Death. A fine subject for sixteen-year-olds!

A. H. And were you then buying contemporary poetry?

J. F. No. My father [Roy Fuller] had lots of poetry I could ransack for what I wanted and I would be given things. My parents gave me a copy of the 1956

Elizabeth Bishop *Selected Poems*, for example, which I thought was wonderful and remember more clearly than anything I had ever bought for myself.

A. H. I've never asked you what it was like starting to be a poet with a distinguished poet for a father. Did you always show him things when you were writing as a teenager?

J. F. The absolute beginnings, negotiation of any embarrassment, I really can't remember, but it very soon became unembarrassing. I showed him my writing and he was always objective and technical and constructive. Whatever idiocies I put in his way, he said really useful things about them and that is a lesson to be learnt when one is oneself encouraging others. I soon felt that I was going my own way, so that I didn't necessarily toe the fatherly line.

A. H. The anxiety of influence would be quite particular in that case.

J. F. Maybe. But I was also in my teens more interested in the films I made. I was more interested in making films and in film itself, interested in wildly eccentric and inexplicable surrealist films.

A. H. Tell me about the films you made.

J. F. They are not worth talking about really, but I used stop-motion in the manner of the Canadian film-maker Norman McLaren a lot of the time, so my characters could move through landscapes with remarkable fluidity and unexpected quirks. I wanted to make films in which almost anything could happen. I liked the surrealist films of Buñuel and Dalí and Man Ray. I don't think my father liked that at all. Later, when I arrived in Oxford, I was surprised to find that my generation was a socialist realist generation, the generation of Ken Loach and so on, but I was always a fantasist. It was the time of *Cathy Come Home* and there I was writing science-fiction plays for television or a play about a lion-faced man on a voyage to Australia to escape his own sense of marginalisation, retiring from the circus and determined to lead an ordinary life, although the passengers faint or even die with terror when he performs. I actually sold that one, but clearly in the context of the TV Wednesday Play it was out of its time. I was then able to do that sort of thing in fiction, so my novels, unlike your own, I may say, are not really novels in the proper sense but fables and fantasies pretty much.

A. H. Reading your earlier books in particular again, the surrealist element is quite strong.

J. F. Well, it might be, and in a way it surfaced again in my novels (the library coming alive in *Flying to Nowhere* for example, or Letty finding the giant Roc in Madagascar in *The Memoirs of Laetitia Horsepole*). As a young writer I was quite ready to be incomprehensible in a way that now I think would be utterly wrong. As I've grown older, the last twenty years or so, I have made an effort to write very, very simply, and that is

from coming to see that the reading world, the reading public who don't read poetry, might be induced to read it if they could be assured it was comprehensible. But as you know, deep down I feel the beauty of poetry is puzzling, isn't really fully comprehensible, at least not until you have paid it quite a bit of attention.

A. H. A formal element which perhaps goes all the way through is the riddle...

J. F. Yes.

A. H. ...or the idea of something presented in a surprising or a mysterious light which a large part of the pleasure of the poem is the solving of...

J. F. Absolutely.

A. H. ...so it's an element of game and play in something that may nonetheless be very serious.

J. F. When I became interested in Augustan poetry, it was an academic interest, to earn my guilty bread at the university, to do research on and so on. But what I was most surprised and pleased to discover was this element of paradox and riddle in poets like Marvell and Pope, particularly Pope with descriptive riddles. Pope can be very surreal, but he is a poet of serious ideas.

A. H. To go back say to the 1940s, early 1950s, surrealism was an element anyway in poetic discourses...

J. F. Yes, but there was terrific reaction from all that, as you know: the poets who were publishing their volumes in the 1950s. I was much younger, and I was just beginning to publish poems in periodicals at the time that the volumes of people like Larkin were coming out, so in a way this was a kind of offered alternative which I pretty firmly turned away from. I wasn't going to be a Movement poet but nor did I quite know what I *was* going to be or what I was going to do. It was at that point that I started reading a lot of the Americans who had done this sort of thing with superb assurance – writers like Wallace Stevens who might seem a kind of quasi-surrealist writer but actually is a deeply philosophical one.

A. H. And of course you went to work in America.

J. F. I went to Buffalo in its pre-Black-Mountain days for a year in 1962. This was the first time I had been to the States. It was interesting to befriend some working poets who I could fit into an American tradition that I only knew from the outside. I was impressed by my friend Saul Touster who I am still in touch with. He is a wonderfully direct poet in the manner of the Lowell of *Life Studies*, roughly speaking, a powerful way of writing which seemed beyond English capabilities, beyond the Movement really.

A. H. You have that wonderful poem, 'My Life on the Margins of Celebrity', where you record what you call true encounters with famous people, including Eliot – though you coyly refuse to disclose what he said.

J. F. Yes, and I am not going to now, either!

A. H. What about Auden, whom you don't mention in that poem?

J. F. People presume because I have written a great tome about him, trying to fathom all his poems, how they work and what they mean, that I knew him very well. He was around in Oxford when I was an undergraduate and we had him to poetry dinners in college, where he might sing 'Take back your mink' from *Pal Joey* and have to be steered back to his rooms, but I didn't know him privately.

A. H. Did he, as he did when he came back in my first year at Oxford, sit somewhere and hope that the young would come to him?

J. F. His reputation was beginning to change in his second visit to Oxford, his public reputation. Back in the 1950s he was under a cloud, he was publishing volumes a lot of people didn't take to. Even *The Shield of Achilles*, which was a wonderful volume, I remember myself thinking was a comedown from *The Orators*, the early stuff that I really had been bowled over by.

A. H. You call him in your new poem the *largest* modern poet...

J. F. He was large-minded. The first poet to print the word 'bugger' and write about the Matchless-Four motorbike, and at the same time to be interested in anthropology and obscure Christian heresies. He took everything on board and the latest volumes of his prose which Edward Mendelson is brilliantly editing at this moment cover an astonishing range.

A. H. Let me take you back to Oxford. You are at New College being taught by John Bayley and David Cecil and Christopher Tolkien. Did you feel encouraged by John in particular as a writer? Was your being a poet part of your relationship with him?

J. F. I don't think it was. He would take a friendly interest in what was going on. He knew that I published things here and there and edited *Isis*, but we rather guarded our activity of that kind from our tutors. I felt that Bayley was on my side, but at the time he was on my side academically, which was much more important, and he was encouraging about what I should read, where I should go, whether I should stay on, whether I got a senior scholarship to fund my research, that kind of thing. It was he who put me on to John Gay. He thought I would like him, and of course I did, because he is full of oddities and riddles. 'The umbrella's oily shed,' things like that, I loved.

A. H. Who were the poet friends you were making at that time? Did you have a sense of a sort of clique of poets at Oxford?

J. F. The playwright Julian Mitchell was then a poet, as many young writers are, though he later became a novelist before he became a playwright. I was friends with him and still am. Dom Moraes was the golden boy of our generation because he had already published his first book with the Parton Press. Peter Levi was a benign and stimulating presence.

A. H. I hadn't realised that you were editor of *Isis*.

J. F. Yes, it was a big thing in those days. You edited it for a term and it appeared every week. Producing a weekly for eight weeks was quite an undertaking. You don't get much academic work done in that term. We published lots of poems. Dennis Potter had a column. All sorts of things went into it and I became bitten by the editing bug so that after I graduated, when I met Ian Hamilton who had had a magazine called *Tomorrow* when he was an undergraduate...

A. H. *Tomorrow*?

J. F. It's a rotten name for a magazine, isn't it? A magazine ought to be about what's happening today. Anyway when he was planning his next magazine (he had an even earlier magazine at school; he was a serial editor), I was interested in helping him to start *the review*.

A. H. What was your role on *the review*?

J. F. I suggested the title itself, from Defoe! The first rather inadequate covers were also my idea because I thought it ought to look like Grigson's *New Verse*, so it had the same sort of typography. That was a mistake...

A. H. It was looking like yesterday rather than...

J. F. Indeed, that's always an error one falls into, it's hard to be absolutely new. I was speaking of Lowell's *Life Studies*: it was the impact of that book which got through to Ian at that time and affected his view of what poetry ought to be like, so he was very choosy. One of my roles was to tout for contributions. I would get poems from all sorts of people that it turned out that Ian, in a rather high-handed way, didn't want, so I had the embarrassing business of going back and saying, 'I begged you for this contribution but sorry, he doesn't want it.' All sorts of people, Redgrove, Peter Levi, Spender, all had to be appeased. Probably I have remained pretty catholic in taste. I was always surprised when the severe Ian showed any sign of softly relenting into publishing anything he didn't really like, like my long Prior-like poem, 'The Art of Love'. I couldn't understand why he published it, it was so totally the sort of poem he hated. I took that as a gesture of friendship.

A. H. We might move on to your coming to Magdalen College. 1966?

J. F. Before that I had done my time in Manchester. As a young lecturer I had had a relatively easy ride in America, though I didn't think so at the time. A lot of Manchester was taken up with finishing off my thesis and acquiring the ability to lecture at the drop of a hat on instructions from John Jump or Frank Kermode on writers like Shelley of whom I knew nothing, so it was a bit of a baptism of fire. I was there for three years.

I got to know a lot of local poets. Glyn Hughes was the most interesting: he died only recently and was writing quite a lot of good poems very bravely up to the point of death. He was young then and we used to meet and I published him and others. Tony Connor is another name that comes to mind and Bernard Bergonzi of course and some other local people in a series of MICA pamphlets – Manchester Institute of Contemporary Art.

A. H. That was a series you established, was it? I am just trying to get a fix on your role as animateur, editor.

J. F. Yes, and I organised poets to come and read. Peter Redgrove needing yet another pint at the eleventh hour. Robert Creeley coming to stay, finding his way from America, various people. Well there was not a great deal of publishing going on, I have to say, but I was learning my trade and, of course, we had come back from America with our daughter Sophie, who was one, and Louisa was then born in Manchester at our first house, so there was a lot of domestic settling going on as well. I didn't publish my second collection until 1967. Those were the years too of *the review* getting going. Ian would come up and stay and we would talk over things.

A. H. How did you first meet Ian Hamilton?

J. F. He wanted me to write for *Tomorrow*, which I did... I wrote a long review of Donald Davie's *Forests of Lithuania* for him and other things. Then I fielded *the review* when I was in the States, getting subscriptions and helping to raise money. There was a long interview with Allen Tate, which (unlike this one) was never published. Tate was another enthusiasm of mine that I couldn't really communicate to Ian.

A. H. Reviewing I don't feel has been a major part of your life? I remember when I was at the *TLS* I badgered you occasionally, I twisted your arm, but...

J. F. I gave up reviewing quite a long time ago. There are two principles. One is you don't need the money so much as you do when you are young, and the other is that it does really tempt one into instant judgements, you show off in reviews and some reviews are more about the reviewer than the book. I didn't want to go on doing that. The principle of only noticing books you admire, which Auden, for example, always held to throughout his life, is admirable. I did a lot of reviewing when I was young, the sort of once-a-month omnium gatherum at the *New Statesman* or the *Listener*.

A. H. Occasional reviewing is really a wonderful way to get on top of some author you have guiltily neglected for a long time.

J. F. Yes. I remember I reviewed Richard Hughes's *Fox in the Attic* and one of the volumes of Evelyn Waugh's *Sword of Honour* Trilogy. I hadn't kept up with those so I had to do my homework. It is all very useful, so I was getting these things properly read and considered. I

have done my share of anthologising, poetry judging and Poetry Book Society choosing and this, that and the other thing, but not *that* much. Some people do a great deal of it. I have been fortunate in having a good academic job, which has given me time to write and I've enjoyed the scholarly side and the teaching side of the work. I have been very lucky. Including ending up with a pension.

A. H. When did you buy the house in North Wales?

J. F. 1969.

A. H. It became a fertile source of poems for you, it became a place to write them. And it also became a place in which you entertained friends and students...

J. F. I am in some sense also partly a Welsh writer! The vacations were long enough for all that. It was true of me, particularly when I started to write novels, that I couldn't keep them going during term times. A vacation is necessary for getting back to a novel you have got on the go, but a vacation is also long enough to have reading parties in Wales and that sort of collaborative existence, which has its own wonderful stimulations to writing. You may remember things that you and I have written to impress each other off the cuff in rather light-hearted circumstances, which we made use of in other ways perfectly seriously. At least that applies to me, maybe not so much to you.

A. H. It perhaps does.

J. F. The University life with its severe demarcations of quite often intense duty, particularly when I was Senior Dean and people were throwing themselves off buildings, or I had to appear in Court to defend them, endless Committees, as well as the teaching: there is no time even for research and certainly not for more reflective modes of writing. I was grateful for the vacations for that and, of course, for sabbatical leave as well, for every seven terms of service, one term off which added to a vacation is quite a few months.

A. H. That is sort of half a year, isn't it?

J. F. Perfect for getting on with what one wants to get on with. But after the mid-1970s, certainly after I had published my first novel, when I nearly always had a novel on the go, the vacations were very useful. I couldn't do what Mark Wormald did when he was an undergraduate here, he got up at six o'clock in the morning, sat down at his Amstrad, and wrote his novel before getting on with his essay. Could you do that?

A. H. No. Had you attempted writing prose fiction before?

J. F. My first adult novel was *Flying to Nowhere*. It was only eighty-five pages but rather cheekily snuck into the Booker shortlist. It's really only a novella. I had written a children's novel and some short stories for children before that. I'd written prose when I was younger, not only those plays but at Oxford little pieces which were, I suppose, a bit like Kafka or something of that sort. They were largely spoken, a bit more putatively like plays in a way. My generation at Oxford was very play-oriented and people like John McGrath, Dennis Potter and Caryl Churchill were all busy being very interested in theatre.

A. H. You hadn't nursed an ambition to be a novelist?

J. F. No, I once started a novel when I was quite young and I didn't think that was the sort of thing I could do, even when I was writing my most novel-like novel, *Tell It Me Again*, which purports to be set in the present and to be psychologically and circumstantially realistic, and I think it is the least interesting of the novels I've written. I've always preferred fantasy and fable.

A. H. *The Burning Boys* drew on your own wartime childhood? It felt to me more personal perhaps...

J. F. It draws a lot on my childhood experience of being evacuated in Blackpool during the war. I accessed that material because it seemed useful for the subject, which is about male rites of passage, about an airman with a damaged face. At its core there's an unrealistic presumption that two separate lives of two quite distinct people can in fiction be significantly brought together, a bit like Virginia Woolf's *Mrs Dalloway*: if she says so then Septimus and Clarissa are connected; but it's a tenuous fiction within the fiction that they are. So *The Burning Boys* was a fable of sorts, a kind of nod to that borrowed structure from Woolf, otherwise full of the gritty detail of Blackpool in the 1940s.

A. H. It has more of that feel of remembered factuality about it than *Look Twice*, the one where they escape by balloon?

J. F. Yes, that was total fantasy.

A. H. It was very beautiful and delightful.

J. F. It was modelled on the *New Arabian Nights* of Robert Louis Stevenson, and those nineteenth-century novels where everybody is telling false stories to each other and the truth of the matter only comes out at the end, like Arthur Machen's *The Three Impostors*. I much enjoyed writing that book and had hopes that somebody might write a screenplay. It would make a wonderful film. That escape in the three-dimensional canvas of the painter, Radim, at the end. But it was not to be.

A. H. At the Florio Society at Magdalen College, to which members submitted their poems anonymously, supposedly, in advance, they were then read during an increasingly drunken evening and analysed...

J. F. Yes, supposedly, because in the days before computers you knew what people's typewritten work looked like.

A. H. Had the Society existed before and been in abeyance? Was it revived by you?

J. F. There is a story that Jon Stallworthy had belonged to it in the late fifties as an undergraduate and it survived in his day, but then it did fall into abeyance and was revived at about my time, maybe shortly before me. You yourself helped to nudge it along...

A. H. I was probably encouraged by you to join it, in my first year, probably in 1972 or 1973, and I remember people like Julian Bell and Andrew McNeillie being there. I can't remember who the secretary was first of all in my time. David Profumo?

J. F. David Profumo was certainly one secretary, I can't remember the order of these things. And then there was this stimulating procession of women secretaries who set wonderful themes. Christiania Whitehead, for example, and Jane Griffiths. Their set subjects cried out to be made into poems.

A. H. This is post-Imlah?

J. F. Mick Imlah was the most creative of all the secretaries. His minutes were entirely self-contained exercises in lunatic fiction, with the members as characters. Florio still goes on. It is my only contact with the college now that I have been retired for fourteen years, but every Sunday evening I go in to the Florio. This is more frequent than in your day, but back then we also had parties and dinners and things. Those have largely been dropped.

A. H. We had Peter Porter to dinner, I remember, and John Bayley and Iris Murdoch. It gave many people a forum they wouldn't otherwise have had and helped a lot of people in ways which have now become more commonplace, perhaps, with teaching writing. But in Oxford there was nothing to compare with it or replace it at the time.

J. F. I'm always careful to distinguish it from teaching. I have always been glad that the Oxford course has never included graded creative writing, to which I feel I have an objection for a number of reasons which we needn't go into. But in its democratic nature Florio is useful to everybody, however practised they feel. I certainly found it very useful myself. If I could see people's eyes glazing over as my poem was produced something was being said.

A. H. I don't expect that happened very often.

J. F. You'd be surprised.

A. H. I always thought it was generous of you to mix in...

J. F. A poem has to take its chances and the surviving anthologies from those days are interesting because you read the poems and it's hard to remember who wrote what. I do remember because I have a particular interest, but it would be vastly puzzling to a literary historian...

A. H. In parallel and sometimes overlapping, there

was the work of the Sycamore Press, which you set up in 1968, two years after you started at Magdalen?

J. F. My wife Prue was given by dear friends a book of typefaces instead of grapes when she had just given birth to our youngest daughter Emily, and that reminded me that I had done some typesetting and printing in the graduate bibliography course on an eighteenth-century flatbed press. It stirred my interest, so we bought an old Arab press and ran it for twenty-five years. Publishing your first book...

A. H. Absolutely, you were my first publisher.

J. F. And Gerard Woodward's first book. There was a moment when you were both in your different ways bathed in the glamour...

A. H. Of the Sycamore Bookers! It is extremely glamorous, looking back through its history now, and for me to have poems I had presented to the Florio Society actually published in a series which included Thom Gunn and Philip Larkin and W. H. Auden was really rather breathtaking.

J. F. That was the idea. We would publish the new, interesting, hitherto unknown poets and we would be able to sell them because subscribers would be able to get books by poets they had heard of as well.

A. H. The big initiating project was James Fenton's?

J. F. Yes, his Newdigate Prize Poem *Our Western Furniture*, about the opening of Japan. It was ambitious. It was imposed in quarto, which is very tricky because you have to get it absolutely right (you can't print all the sheets and then find they don't fold to produce the correct sequence of sonnets) but we managed it.

A. H. There was a hardback edition as well, wasn't there, in a special binding...

J. F. Yes, Prue had been doing some book binding up at the Polytechnic, Brookes as it is now. She bound a dozen copies of James's book and Norman Bryson's poems as well. It was good to produce a hardback with a dust jacket.

A. H. James was a pupil of yours?

J. F. He read English for a time, and took Prelims. I remember talking with him about Milton. He then changed to PPE. He became a very good friend and we have collaborated on a lot of things, translated *Seven Deadly Sins* by Brecht and Weill together, published a book of poems together.

A. H. You published *Partingtime Hall*, a book of thoroughly scurrilous poems. His first book was a wonderfully auspicious beginning to the press's life, wasn't it?

J. F. Yes, it was really. I sent a copy of *Our Western Furniture* to George MacBeth who was a BBC producer and it was read on the radio... By James, if I recollect.

A. H. And the press was a wonderful way of binding in pupils, friends, people from the larger literary world outside Oxford, it seemed to be a marvellous sort of focus... It was absolutely magical to come into.

J. F. Undergraduates would come along to set and print their own poems but if they came on a weekend when we were doing an unknown poem by Philip Larkin they would be set to work on that. With a vodkatini.

A. H. What led you to end its operations twenty-five years later? Maybe a small press is finite?

J. F. We had done it for long enough, I don't think there were any particular reasons.

A. H. Did it make money?

J. F. None at all.

A. H. Did you lose money?

J. F. No. At one time I was perhaps foolishly hoping that it might make money, but I was concerned that it shouldn't, just so it wouldn't become something I had to say anything about in my tax returns. Absolutely no danger of that! Anybody who runs such a venture now will know that very well. Of course with the internet now it is possible to have a sales and publicity network which does work. One of my books has been published by a new little press, the Emma Press, run by Emma Wright, and she is wonderfully well organised. In the days of the Sycamore Press sales could only be achieved by going down to the Charing Cross Road with a briefcase full of the physical objects and trying to get them put on sale.

A. H. It was much more akin to the world of small magazine publishing, wasn't it? I remember Jon Silkin coming round the King's Arms with copies of *Stand*. It had a sort of romance that things online don't have.

J. F. I remember sending Jon Silkin poems back in 1954 when *Stand* had only just started, and going to visit him. He wasn't in, so his wife gave me a cup of tea and he came back exhausted with a knapsack full of unsold *Stands*.

A. H. Fiction. You say in your new long poem that poetry needs a narrative drive. I think you mean the long poem, but you've written long verse narratives on a number of occasions?

J. F. I can see that short poems don't need a narrative drive. I suppose I could extend the claim to hope that short poems can sometimes have fictional circumstances akin to the narrative in a way, in the Browning manner. And discovering Browning through the requirements of the new syllabus after 1972 and having to teach him was very stimulating to me.

A. H. You really hadn't looked at him much before?

J. F. I didn't know the long works. I knew the obvious

things, things people even today will tend to know. But many of the longer poems are quite difficult, they need a lot of appetite and attention. And that had to be given by undergraduates taking the Tennyson and Browning paper and of course their poor tutor had to be in advance of them. But Browning showed that even short poems have to have something like narrative drive. Think of a poem like 'My Last Duchess': it's in a sense a static tableau, but it still has narrative implications to explore, proleptically as it were, or analeptically one should say. But indeed, yes, I had written a long poem about a transvestite and an art forger, the poem set in the modern world in the Pushkin stanza (fourteen lines of rhymed octosyllabics). I had written that shortly before writing my first novel, which I thought of as just another narrative work that happened to be in prose, whereas *The Illusionists* was in Pushkin stanzas.

A. H. The Pushkin stanza was rather in the air at that moment, I remember, wasn't it? Andrew Waterman wrote a long poem in the Pushkin stanza.

J. F. He did. It was published in 1981. *The Illusionists* was published in 1980. We must have been writing them at the same time. I think it was Charles Johnston's translation of *Eugene Onegin* that sparked me. I was interested to know why Babette Deutsch's translation in Penguin was suddenly dropped and replaced with Charles Johnston's when I thought hers was actually better or at least perfectly good.

A. H. Was the Johnston thought to be more accurate? I remember it being acclaimed when it came out.

J. F. My daughter, Sophie, who read Russian, kindly gave me an afternoon where we compared stanzas and looked to see and I don't think that was the case at all. I think it was just a fresh translator's voice and a matter of fashion, Penguin's feeling that the existing Deutsch must be out of date. But it's not necessarily true.

A. H. I read the sixth chapter of *The Illusionists* again after I had finished *The Bone Flowers*: the wonderful dream or looking-glass world of palindromic names, it is fantastically entertaining. It made me wonder (thinking about both those poems) what your strategy is for writing a book-length poem? Do you plan the narrative very closely in advance, do you have an overall scheme for it when you begin?

J. F. I have to have a brief outline of a story, which has a circumstance and a resolution. You have to have an ending. But poems of this sort are written in such a way that they allow infinite digressions. The story can hang fire for page after page while something else goes on, and of course the new poem, *The Bone Flowers*, is exactly the same.

A. H. The narrative is less developed there because they both turn on matters of a sort of forgery or imposture. There are Shakespearean sonnets, which are clever as pastiches. They are cleverly undermined by the poem itself questioning their possible validity.

J. F. Do you think that if the poem says they are, or suggests they are, utter forgeries, that the reader might think, 'well perhaps they might not be'? Well, they are intended to be the sort of sonnets Shakespeare might have written if he had written sonnets about a Greek myth instead of sonnets about the Dark Lady and the Beautiful Youth. So, yes, pure pastiche but doubt is cast on them because the hero who speaks up for them is involved in shady dealings in the art world anyway, that's a part of what Billy Emerald is like.

A. H. There is that satirical element, part of the Augustan mode engaging satirically with the contemporary world. It recurs all the way through actually.

J. F. It may have been liberating for me to read Gay and Pope all those years ago and to realise that one can write directly about the fat cats of this world, one can even name them if one wants to.

A. H. Well you did it also in a way I suppose in *Epistles to Several Persons*, didn't you, using the Burns stanza, and the recipients were people in different worlds from the academic?

J. F. It allowed me in my probably greatly misinformed way to sound off about my prejudices in music or whatever. If I don't like Stockhausen I can say so in a poem.

A. H. It is just an extraordinary experience reading through your poems again that so many phrases from them are completely welded into my consciousness...

J. F. That is very charming of you to say so...

A. H. It was remarkable: it was like the memories that music brings back, they were marvellous in themselves and they were evocative of so much else. And now we have *The Bone Flowers*.

J. F. Well, that is meant to be fun, too, the sort of poem that can include anything that swims into view. Including a lot about music.

A. H. But it is really about age, debility and death.

J. F. Yes, and about the superstitions associated with hypochondria and one's fear of hypochondria as much as fear of death. I hope it's slightly tongue-in-cheek about death. One shouldn't be too solemn.

A. H. It has become a wonderful analysis of feelings about diminishing with time and...

J. F. If you feel as I do, that poems are a way of retaining the sense of how one has felt in life about things, much as some people take photographs, to write poems is to preserve something of what life has been, then obviously the sense of losing must be very much a part of how one writes this sort of poem. I suppose there is an elegiac feel to a lot of it.

A. H. Elegiac, and celebratory...

J. F. Yes, that as well. Both these things, and very often we can do both of them at the same time, as it were, to qualify each other.

A. H. Do you have a sense of putting off some poems?

J. F. One or two things I've written have been around ideas that I know I want to do but I haven't yet done. They may just have needed a bit more germination in terms of what form they took, but not often. I think normally I write the next thing that seems to be brilliantly to hand, you know. It is there looking at me and I nod at it and take it up.

A. H. Thinking of this idea of writing poems being in a very complex way a sort of noting of what is happening to one as one goes through one's life, you have always been quite productive and you have become more productive since you retired from teaching...

J. F. There is always a danger of writing too much, or wasting a subject (to go back to what you were saying a minute ago), wasting it before the time is right, and you think 'I could have written about it better now'. But patience and restraint are useful virtues here.

A. H. Does a day ever pass without your turning some sensation or perception into a verbal or potentially poetic form?

J. F. I do keep a notebook without which I would lose a lot of ideas. And that is one of my major pieces of advice to anybody who writes: to get it down. The worst thing in the world is to think, 'Yesterday I had this idea, what was it?' Absolutely lost. Writing is not just unscrewing the fountain pen at the desk and settling down for the daily grind, it is being alert to fleeting perceptions.

A. H. I think I am right in saying that in all your – is it – twenty-five collections, you have never written a poem in free verse?

J. F. That's a very interesting question. I have written a whole book without using rhyme, I have certainly written lines of randomly uneven length but not necessarily without the occasional securing rhyme. I have recently published a collection of prose poems. But you might be right, yes, you might well be right.

A. H. I just feel that form is crucial to you. Does the form in a sense generate the poem? How fast do you write poems in for instance the quite exacting measure of *The Bone Flowers*?

J. F. Ottava rima, you mean? It is hard, I admit. I tried to think of George Gordon idling at his mantelpiece with his hock-and-seltzer and producing hundreds of stanzas. I tended to go at it in short bursts so there are identifiable sequences of thought within it or ideas carried on from stanza to stanza. Or purely narrative stanzas which advance the story. For instance I had to summarise the borrowed story of the appointment in Samarra at one point. I wanted to get it in, so it was quite a task, though it only covers about three stanzas. I can do that in a day easily. Or at least enough to refine it the next day. It is tough in ottava rima because you can't have rhyme words which draw too much attention to themselves or you get stuck. It's rather like writing limericks, a good limerick survives on your using the only three possible but tricky rhymes that you need and no others and these work beautifully together. That problem is more severe with ottava rima. It is easier to use rather easy mild rhyme words but on the other hand that can make for a slightly bland texture...

A. H. There is a lot of ironic humour to be got out of rhyme...

J. F. Yes, so if, as I do, I rhyme Cambridge with Beryl Bainbridge, I am pleased because that seems a necessary thing, it is crying out to be done somewhere in writing. But it is one of the most taxing aspects of verse. Hopkins is responsible for keeping alive the perfectly forgettable agricultural word 'sillion' which means a furrow, you know? If you have vermillion and million what else could you do: you need sillion. You have to avoid those contortions. Hopkins doesn't really avoid them and Browning doesn't either, he cheerfully tackles them head on.

A. H. What about librettos: you have written one for Nicola LeFanu, *Dream Hunter*.

J. F. It is one kind of collaboration, which I much enjoy. Nicola has a new BBC commission next year at the Barbican with words by me about the mutual situation of siege in Gaza. I once worked a lot with Bryan Kelly on writing jolly music for children. I also wrote a Hymn to the Senses for Robin Holloway that was done at a Prom. You can't hear the words, a massed choir... the music is wonderful but you don't hear any of the words.

A. H. When you have made selections from your poems, what did you feel you were doing, were you cutting something out or refining an idea of your verse which you preferred?

J. F. Well, when I did a *Collected Poems* I did go through everything and try to leave out a lot of stuff I didn't think worked for one reason or another, cutting out a bit of dead wood. But largely I did include everything, even things I could barely remember writing or felt suspicious about my aims or skill in writing them. But that was quite a fat book. Then when I came to do my two *Selected Poems*, in particular the more recent one, *New Selected Poems 1983–2008*, I simply wanted to give a representative sense of what I had done in my previous eight collections. I knew I couldn't include everything. I only put in one of my longer poems, 'Star Gazing'. I didn't include other long ones like 'Round and Round' or 'The Grey and the Green'. There wouldn't be space. It had to be a handleable volume. It had been some time since I'd had a collection of that sort and it was to represent me to a new generation of readers. So yes, aiming at representation, really.

A. H. A *Selected Poems* tend to favour the shorter poem. The long tend to unbalance. But 'Star Gazing' is a wonderful poem. You wrote it around the deaths of your parents.

J. F. Yes. And it is saturated in the landscape (and skyscape) of Corsica, where for many years we would spend the summers.

A. H. If you were to do a *Selected Poems* for your whole career now? What I am getting at is something writers rarely talk about: how they themselves see their whole *oeuvre,* which perhaps…

J. F. One can become very tired of some old poems. I won't say old familiar poems because there is a true sense in which one after a while can't bear ever to look at them again. I am not constantly re-reading my stuff, but I know that when I last looked at poem A, poem B, whatever it might be, I thought, *okay I can remember what sort of a person I was then, what I was like.* I can now see with a lot of maturity and hindsight what sort of poem it is and you think, *well it would have passed muster in 1959, or 1968, or 1977 or 1986,* I am inventing dates here, and it is a long stretch of time for one to have any kind of loyalty to the things that one has written. If I was doing an overall *Selected* I might be quite savage. I would need a bit of advice maybe from some reliable person like yourself, but I would really winnow, because after all readers don't have time. There's such a lot of poetry about, poets should publish less, probably. Poets should publish less and better, cross their fingers hoping for an audience, but not bombard the world with stuff that isn't of the best.

A. H. But that suggests that one would knowingly publish something which one thought wasn't so good, but I think you are suggesting that retrospect…

J. F. You think it's good at the time, but it may not last, it may be like a bad vintage of wine that is overpowered by its tannins or it just doesn't have any oomph.

A. H. So the selecting process might be beneficial in just preserving? It has two duties: to preserve the best poems and to give a representative picture of the career of the writer?

J. F. Yes.

A. H. They may not precisely be the same thing.

J. F. Of course, when one edits another poet, as it sometimes happens that very special onerous task is bestowed upon one, it is a grave responsibility.

A. H. You did a selection of Auden's, didn't you. It must have been very difficult to do that?

J. F. Oh yes, such a bountiful writer and I had only a hundred pages. I chose a method that I thought Auden himself might have been amused by which was to have one poem from every year of his writing life.

A. H. I don't think I quite took that in.

J. F. You might think it is a silly thing to do but actually it does give you the spread and it does begin to tell you when he was in a really low patch, you know. There were some years (like, I think, 1950) when you really feel there is not much going on, so I fiddled that poem-for-every-year-of-his-writing-life idea a little bit, I tweaked it just slightly so as not to edge out the poems from the very rich periods, you know? 1938: you could fill the whole book with 1938, so I cheated a little bit. But that seemed one way of doing it.

A. H. What else have you selected?

J. F. I did Pope in that same series.

A. H. That is difficult for someone who generally writes very long poems?

J. F. Yes it is, it is. Did I include the whole of *The Rape of the Lock*? I rather hope I did.

A. H. Yes, you did.

J. F. And even if I didn't I might have done, if you see what I mean. In Pope's case I wanted to pretend that he didn't always write in the way people expected, so I did include some of the ballads and things just to make it not too forbidding to the reader who finds heroic couplets difficult to read, though God knows they aren't difficult to read, but some people are put off…

Five Poems

JOHN FULLER

Fulehung

The Fulehung like a lunatic
With a bouncing bladder on a stick
Runs through the streets of Thun.
Its mask is horned, its mouth a slit,
Half terror, half buffoon.
There is no stopping it.

The memory of where I stood
In those deserted streets
Beneath an icy demilune
Comes back to me, for though
I ran as hard as ever I could,
I did not stir á foot.

The Fulehung will find me
In the silent shadowed square.
The Fulehung will find me
Although I am not there.
The Fulehung is behind me,
Its nose a bulb of blood.

The face that groans in the stomach,
The eyes that ache like a cave,
The mask that stares from the mirror,
The lips that never forgave
Are all that define the Fulehung,
Who's there to make me behave.

Down my back the discs were strung,
Into my arms the hinges put,
My legs locked in their sockets:
I cannot run forever through my life
With bones that cry out to the skies
And nothing in my pockets.

I'd licked the ink to play the fool
And legends stained my tongue.
I waited in the midnight room
With its clump of fallen soot
And silent stood the Fulehung.
Silent stood the ghoul.

I cannot run, and yet I run
More than I ever did
When half in terror, half in play,
Panting, I stopped and hid.
Now in the gradual dwindling of the day
I run, but cannot run.

The Fulehung has found me
With its bladder and its grin
In the lava-flow of my desires,
Where standing pools and turgid fires
And silence's ecstatic din
Are all around me.

My ribs are like a ladder
On which my heart took fright.
I look upon my life in fear,
As if from unaccustomed height
Where everything at last is clear:
The Fulehung has found me.

Trawling

So fine a net, we thought
    It could not fail.
All night – uncertainty!
    Trawling for revelation
    With lowered sail,
And the long skeins unfolding
    Into the sea.

Our quest – more than a question
    Idly asked and answered,
More than appraisal of the best
    That makes the best what it is,
    And more than mere chance:
Again and again we hurl our nets,
And over the oily waves
    The lanterns dance.

There is an art in judging
    The fineness of a mesh
    That sweeps and winnows.
We think the weave is coarse enough
    To leave the waste behind:
It is like the still ponds of our youth
Where we sat all day in the sun
    And what did we find?
We hoped for astonishing monsters
    And brought up minnows.

Talk or Walk

The good Doctor couldn't put
His left foot (or was it his right
Foot?) forward to walk into a room.
He simply couldn't choose.
Was it diffidence?
Was it inhibition?

He couldn't walk from a room either.
Once he had started to talk,
Out-talking the competition,
Laying down the law,
Holding the floor,
All was well. But then?

He would hover at the threshold,
Jerking and twitching,
While everyone waited.
The bookseller's son translated
From provincial Lichfield
To the drawing rooms of the literati.

When we are put at our unease
And have no idea how to behave,
We either stay, anxious to please
(Which cheek? Which knife?),
Maintaining our position,
Or we walk.

Yes, we would like to leave.
We tread the priceless Turkey carpet,
Noticing the labour of its weave.
What can we possibly say?
We are not all like the good Doctor.
Easy for him to talk.

Sometimes I feel like getting permission
To avoid this altogether and simply
Click on the walkthrough of my life.

In Whose Head?

Schumann, op. 41, no. 2.

When at last in old age I listen again
To the music of my youth, finally it speaks
Nothing to me of my father, who shared it with me
(That lilt in the second movement, for example, something
Like a folk-song, almost a fore-echo of Richard Strauss).
It is familiar to me only as itself, nothing else.
I am inside the head of its begetter, not my own,
And yet its sound over the years, hasn't it changed?
Not just the somewhat unlikely tempo of these players,
But the whole charge and depth of its lucid argument?
Surely it has, for why now would it make me weep?

Too Late

I dreamed I lay asleep beside you.
It was too late to touch you, or call out.

The bees were pulling at the roses, and
Some cloud stuff stretching in the summer air.

My mind was capable of thoughts.
My position had a familiar feel.

My mind knew what it was about.
My shape knew nothing but itself.

I longed to wake and find you, but
I could not move. I could not stir my hand.

My body was a ghost of sorts,
Knowing where it was. It was elsewhere,

Some bird or other gave a shout,
Intending to call the day to order.

But nothing was happening, and nothing more,
It seemed, was ever going to happen.

I could not stir my hand to let you know
That I was there. I could not stir.

Just for that moment there was no future,
No hope at all of going back.

No memory of whatever brought me there,
Though I knew it was my entire life.

I longed to turn and see you,
To let you know I hadn't gone away.

But all the weight of me was in the chair
Where I was fast asleep. You were not there.

John Fuller at Eighty: The Florio Society

Tom Cook

AMONG OTHER THINGS, I owe John Fuller my love of high-quality paper. That's not a sentence I would've imagined myself writing in 2010, aged seventeen, when I first read his name in Christopher Hitchens's memoirs. (Good paper featured there, too, in stories about the Sycamore Press's very limited-edition pamphlets of explicit verse.) Nor would I have guessed that my copy of his *New Selected Poems*, bought at that time, would have ended up inscribed by him in a dauntingly ornate room in Oxford. The surrealism was not eased by the fact that, the first time I met him, John was seated directly beneath his own portrait...

Magdalen's summer common room, home to most of the John Florio Society's meetings during my time at Oxford, I now think of a welcoming place, and the alignment of the other John F. with his wall-hung likeness turned out to be a coincidence of seating arrangements; his is one among many depicting the college's celebrated fellows, including the former Professor of Poetry, Seamus Heaney. (I had worried that some arcane Oxford law meant Fuller *had* to be enthroned in this terrifying tribute to himself: a high-end repeat of a pub I once visited in Humberside, where regulars sat beneath their own oil portraits.)

*

The Florio, which John has helped steer since the 1970s, is aware of tradition. Meeting each week of the Oxford term, the society's round-table format has encouraged the work of dozens of noted poets since its inception, including Bernard O'Donoghue, Mick Imlah, Jon Stallworthy and James Fenton. Poems are presented anonymously, and depending on attendance will receive comment from something like five to twenty people. Some, like John and myself, are primarily poets, while others are mainly critics, and the discussion is varied and searching. What's always seemed remarkable to me is that, despite the weight of technical and academic knowledge in the room, poems are taken on their own terms; wine flows, at Christmas time or on a birthday there is cake, and sometimes the conversation falls down deep political, historical or literary rabbit-holes for long periods, but ultimately the focus is on the work, and no amount of knowledge or tradition is allowed to compensate for a poem that's unsure of itself. The longest and best debates have been over apparently small things – syntax, punctuation, rhythm – which, the more they're looked at, emerge as the essential elements.

The attention to detail, the granting of poetry's importance and mysterious nature while also refusing to be cowed by it, the willingness to take the poem down a peg – technically, stylistically, even morally – before building it back up into a finished work of art: these are some of the greatest strengths of John's poetry, and the core of his importance to other writers. John was only the second real poet I'd ever met when I first arrived in Oxford (the first was David Wheatley, who had taught me at Hull). I eventually risked soliciting his comments on a few of my poems. When they came, they were cuttingly honest.

Had I been just a little younger I might've despaired. Already in agreement with him about the need for form, rhythm and music in a poem, John's real value as a teacher for me lies in his ability to challenge: far from receiving reinforcement of my love of form, many times I have sent him what I've thought is a poem with carefully developed images or emotions – only for him to point out, ever so mildly, that a major part of its construction is misplaced in some way, so that far from soaring, my creation will remain stranded on the runway leaking oil until I sort things out. Balanced as they were with warm encouragement of what was working, his views on what wasn't became invaluable in my shakier early days.

Even in my few years as an attending student, the Society took repeated new approaches to writing: sometimes offering writing prompts and themes, sometimes shedding anonymity, sometimes collapsing into sheer childishness and giggling. But for all those changes, its central concern with the importance of poetry – no matter how it varies or seems to have gone astray to some – remained constant. What the Florio creates, then, is a point of stability in a city always in flux. Poets come and go, attendance waxes and wanes, but for decades now there has always been a Florio Society, and for as long as there has been a Florio Society, there has been a John Fuller at its heart. Absent only for family holidays and the odd professional engagement, he is quietly but constantly available to the university's young poets – even those who, the first time they met him, drank far more than their share of the circulating wine to calm their nerves.

*

Each Christmas, John produces something new: a complex word-search quiz hidden within a cryptic poem, or, as last year, a little pamphlet of funny double dactyl poems taking aim at literary and political figures from across the ages – each carefully designed and typeset, printed on laid paper, sewn up by hand, and distributed to friends and acquaintances. Nowadays the pamphlets come from a desktop printer, the Sycamore Press having retired just before I was born; but the scrupulousness and the delight in a made thing done well are the same as they ever were.

When I first knew him, one of the stories I was most keen to hear from John first-hand was about Philip Larkin. The Press had published him in its fascinating *Sycamore Broadsheets* series – a subscription-based run of pamphlets featuring the work not only of major poets like Larkin and Thom Gunn, but also introducing readers to younger or lesser-known authors such as James Fenton or the Pennine poet Glyn Hughes (whose work has sadly begun to fall from readership in the years since his death in 2011 – something I think a great shame, and not just because he wrote so beautifully about the landscape I grew up in). Larkin had already seen the appeal of the small presses – the Hessle-based Marvell Press had launched his extraordinary collection *The Less Deceived* straight into the public consciousness – and agreed to a *Broadsheets* edition of his Baudelaire imitation 'Femme Damnées', proof that he had liked at least one 'foreign poem', he confessed. It seemed, and seems, magical to me that mere dedication to and love of poetry could produce such an extraordinary line of publications, without the need for teams of designers, marketers and distributors. The best place to read about the Press, of course, is Ryan Roberts's book *John Fuller and the Sycamore Press*, a compilation of letters and prose contributions from authors, as well as a long interview with John.

It was off the back of such conversations that I sought his advice about paper earlier this year. Not the most exciting topic in the world, I nonetheless needed tips on how to publish an elegy I'd written in memory of a beloved former teacher, which my old school had asked for copies of, and which I felt ought to be done with more care than a print-on-demand website could offer. I was delighted when, over lunch and a few ensuing emails, John unfolded a warm, enthusiastic step-by-step guide to all the fiddly processes I knew nothing about: collating pages; choosing a binding; the grammage of paper; the pros and cons of vellum, laid and smooth; the difficulties of getting desktop ink to remain unsmudged on textured card for the covers. Best of all, he saved me a fortune simply by knowing which products were too crap to bother with; I would almost certainly have fallen foul, for example, of the store-brand 'luxury' paper, had he not advised me to check how translucent it was in the pack, ignoring its official weight. He answered my stupid questions with good humour, downplaying the impressiveness of the Sycamore years, but clearly drawing on a vast reserve of publishing knowledge. And he insisted on buying my lunch while doing it.

*

The title poem of John's most recent book, *Gravel in My Shoe*, is part of a sequence about a strange Welsh healer-woman born in the late 1860s, but its closing lines have the timelessness I associate with all truly meaningful poetry:

> Adventure is required, to go where
> The heart says you belong.
> Which might be anywhere – or nowhere.
> I doubt it could be wrong.
>
> The only peace: to know my place
> And what I now must do,
> Striding with the light full in my face,
> And gravel in my shoe.

As well as being timeless, it is universal: in that little lyrical moment, the speaker could be anyone else as much as the mysterious, roaming Mary Price. The sequence ends with a little poem called 'When', in which we are reminded that 'We are both themes / From one song-book, / Leaves from a single tree.' On the page opposite, a more personal poem reminds a friend of 'Chasing our shadows in a vain endeavour / To tell the world that we would last forever', striking a self-elegiac note. The whole book, in fact, is filled with poems written by a man looking and feeling back through an extraordinary life, and what he says of poems is also true of his other creations – the legacies of the Sycamore Press and the Florio Society, the immeasurable collective gratitude of young people who have benefited from his generosity:

> Life is too short, but poetry's eternal.

Strike a Light

Andrew McNeillie

IT WAS EARLY in December, 1969, that I first met John Fuller. One of those startling bright winter mornings, cold and clear, that cities sometimes surprise you with and which Oxford can stage so well. Was the light still in my eyes? Emrys Jones tugged the long curtain one way, John tugged it the other, while I sat opposite them sunk in a sofa, now squinting, now shielding my eyes with a hand. The whole business of putting out the sun seemed to take forever. I suppose it helped break the ice. Then Emrys folded himself back into his chair like some strange umbrella with not enough spokes and a quizzical handle. He was begowned for the occasion. I don't recall that John was. Perhaps I was too preoccupied by his polo-neck sweater, cavalry-twill trousers, red socks and suede shoes, to notice. My wardrobe was far more basic and I suppose it interested me to see how different sartorial arrangements might be. I hadn't done any homework on John Fuller. But I was more than aware of his poems, those early, sharp, dark poems which I still love especially; and I think I was a little nervous of their author. My introduction to them came courtesy of Alvarez, in both the original and revised version of *The New Poetry*. These were still quite early days for the poet.

Pleasantries over and the sun eclipsed, we sat looking at each other. That too seemed to take forever. I can't remember how we got underway, insofar as we did at all. But something had to give. I was being interviewed for an undergraduate place at Magdalen College – to read English, of course. I couldn't claim to be fit for anything else. It was 1969 and I was twenty-three years old. Not long before I had spent just short of a year living alone in some hardship on the Aran Islands. I had sat no exam to get me to this point, but before going to Aran I had been a sub-editor in the BBC's Radio Newsroom in London, along with fast-track graduates from Cambridge like John Simpson and Will Wyatt. I was a graduate of local newspapers in the South Wales valleys. I was as good as them at what I had to do but I hardly had their self-confidence.

Emrys and John, at this time, liked to take in an 'oddball' candidate, someone who'd not come up the conventional way, and they admitted one a year to their eight, if they could. It said everything about the social and intellectual alignment of these men. The practice was opposed by some of the Fellowship and while it outlasted me, I don't think it outlasted my successor who seemed to have fooled around a little and he sounded its death-knell. Any such arrangement would probably cause outrage in today's press were it to be introduced now, straight 'A's and a CV pure as the driven snow being the order of the day. I was told about this 'scheme' and put my case in a lengthy letter, in the first instance, to Emrys.

More than a little to my surprise I was invited for interview. '... I have to make it clear,' I can still hear myself saying, perhaps once, perhaps twice, to these steadily observant and slightly mysterious gentlemen, 'I have not done any *systematic* reading.' What had I been reading? I don't know what I said. I suspect it was something general, about authors I liked: Synge, Yeats, Joyce, Flann O'Brien, Dylan Thomas, Baudelaire... Perhaps I mentioned books I'd been reading on the island, when not too busy fishing. I'd read *Middlemarch* there and been bowled over by it. I'd read Hardy's *Return of the Native.* But the novelists were never my baby and they wouldn't have taken me far that morning. I'd also been reading Geoffrey Hill's *King Log* and Richard Murphy's *Sailing to an Island.* John began to grow a little twitchy. That I do remember clearly. I summoned up Synge. He was the one responsible for my going to Aran in the first place. I spoke about Synge's English and the Irish language, saying it was undoubtedly a poetic language...

'What did I mean by that,' John pounced.

What did I mean? I had one example up my sleeve and I think it saved my bacon. 'If you are an Aran man and you want a light for a cigarette, you ask: *an bhfuil deargadh a'd*...' Emrys, looking slightly startled, uncrossed his legs and crossed them again, somehow earnestly, clearing his throat at the same time. John watched me steadily... 'which is to ask, "do you have a reddener", that is, something to redden the end of the cigarette. Now, that is surely a poetic way of thinking...' I had a couple of other examples. But that, it seemed, was enough. After a few pleasantries these two very brilliant and, to me, inscrutable men showed me the door.

That was that. 'Fiasco...' I said to myself, as I left Magdalen's decidedly old New Buildings under no illusions as to my hopeless performance. Little did I know that I would quite often say the same as I left that building in the coming three years (once, as I remember vividly, after John had told me I must cultivate my *amour-propre*). He saw straight into me, or so it felt; and so he would on many another occasions. So I learned from him, and still do. They wrote in February offering me a place. You could have knocked me down with a cigarette paper. It was the best piece of good luck I ever had. As I could hardly have guessed then, it was the first step towards what has become the truest friendship. John has many startling gifts. His gift for friendship is not the least of them. Of course poetry is at the heart of it – how could it not be with such a man? – but there is everything else that makes up friendship too. Poetry alone is not enough (as if poetry could be alone, and not, as it must be, enmeshed in everyday life, thought and care).

Oxford in those three years more or less killed my muse inasmuch as I had one. If a muse might be killed, shed not a tear, I say. Would-be poets are two-a-penny and cheaper by the dozen in Oxford. I did not go to the college's Florio Society meetings. These were of course special, intimate occasions. Bernard O'Donoghue, who arrived to teach medieval literature at Magdalen in my second year, and who is the other vital lifeline in my story, is one of the Florio's most prestigious graduates, along with Mick Imlah and the great James Fenton, an extraordinary presence in my time. I did go out to the garage at Benson Place and saw the Arab printing press in action. If you'd have told me then that I would inherit it and house it in my own garage, I certainly would not have believed you. I went with my wife to parties and dinner parties with John and Prue and met poets – Anthony Thwaite, Peter Scupham, Peter Levi, Peter Porter – and had enjoyable glimpses into John's world. But I would soon be summoned by Bells, to go to work editing Virginia Woolf, and Oxford would fall far away from my life.

Thirteen years later I returned to work there in publishing. I also set up the Clutag Press and have now published John and quite a few others: Hill, Heaney, Imlah, and Paulin among them. It was a continuation of the Sycamore Press by other means and with other (archipelagic) causes. But John and Sycamore had been the catalyst, the living proof it might be done, the match that reddened the fuse.

*

Fast-forward. Suppose you find yourself sitting down to lunch at Pierre Victoire, an inexpensive brasserie on Oxford's Little Clarendon Street. It won't be long before you realise there are three strange old men in the corner, making a spectacle of themselves, talking a lot, drinking red wine, laughing together, and eventually shuffling pieces of paper between them. Now they are silent and serious as they read. Now one starts up. Then the other. Round the table they go, and once more, at least three times. What is this vinous symposium? I'll tell you. It's a meeting of the Senile Florio Society (SFS). Come again next month and the month after and you'll see it in action again, if action is the word. The late Jon Stallworthy was briefly a member, in an honorary kind of way. But otherwise it's exclusively the triumvirs of Fuller, O'Donoghue, and the man with a reddener. For me it is a master class with two masters. We circulate a poem, two perhaps, by email in advance. Then each is discussed, each line, each word and phrase submitted to extreme tests, driven almost always by John's forensic logic and softened by Bernard's extraordinary version of negative capability. John's insistence on logicality as a starting point, a baseline, can seem almost illogical, given the nature of poetry. But it is far from that. Hard as it can be to take, it never fails to improve a poem or to expose a failure for what it is. I'm addicted to these occasions now. I think we all three are and pine for them during the long summer holidays. My writing has been improved by them beyond measure. I write now with a sharper eye and ear to all the elements that give a piece of writing its difference. John Fuller never sets himself above us, though above us he most surely is, a man of lightning intellectual celerity and vast knowledge. Yet he needs and values his friends as we all do, and this is the major part of his essential magic, this and his absolute passion for poetry. It is what has underwritten all the sway he has held over generations of writers – Fenton, Hollingshurst, Imlah, O'Donoghue, and many others – at Magdalen and in Benson Place, and now also one lesser light at Pierre Victoire.

John

Jane Griffiths

To begin by saying that when I think of John I think of grids will hardly sound like a compliment – but it rather depends on the grids. There was the chess board in the corner of his college room, and his occasional mention of a particularly challenging move, sent by post. There was the over-life-sized chess-board of Otmoor: the landscape that Lewis Carroll wrote into *Alice through the Looking-Glass*. There were sestinas, black on white squares of six-by-six lines with a three-line tail. There were printers' type-trays and their apparently nonsensical, practically logical divisions. There was symbolic logic; that is, more Carroll. There were sestinas made up entirely of lines from Carroll's *Symbolic Logic*. There were quads, of course, and although this may be memory playing false, I'd instinctively say New Buildings II:2 was a perfect cube. Certainly the ceiling was high enough for my twelve-foot rowing boat to be stored there, resting on its stern just inside the door. John said: 'My scout will wonder what it's for'; why precisely we put it there escapes me, but I do remember carrying it from the river across the lawn while a visiting friend from Christ Church looked on in horror.

As for why it's that, particularly, that comes to mind – well, it goes back to the question John asked during admissions, when for some reason candidates were put in a rocking chair, and because I was still recovering from the flu his voice seemed to be coming from somewhere near that very high ceiling: 'Surely you don't mean to imply that Oscar Wilde was flippant?' To which the only possible reply was 'Yes ... NO', catapulting forward in the chair and very nearly out of it, while half articulating something about its being a performance to make what mattered seem as if it didn't – which at seventeen and only recently escaped from small-town Holland, I understood purely in the abstract. A couple of years later, there was the boat.

Though not only the boat, of course. There can't have been many tutors to whom it would have been possible to say 'I'm stencilling my curtains with spray paint' in confidence that this would be thought an entirely sensible way of spending a morning. There can't have been many who would send a (pre-email) note not on college stationery but on a yellow and orange and cornflower-blue-blotched piece of hand-made paper with the caption 'lousy example of experimental silk-screen printing'. There certainly weren't many who kept trays of type in their study and a printing press in their garage; who invited us over to help with typesetting; who showed that writing, printing, publishing and messing around with paint were at least as much part of life as essay-writing, and that there weren't strict boundaries between them. 'The world is everything that is the cat', as I would have sworn John once said – in 'Interrogations'? – but apparently didn't, or no longer does. Auden (of course) did say that 'If an undergraduate announces to his tutor one morning that Gertrude Stein is the greatest writer who ever lived [...] he is really only saying something like this: "I don't know what to write yet or how, but yesterday while reading Gertrude Stein I thought I saw a clue" [...].' There was something in the very rich mix of John's writing, tutoring, printing, talking, and heading off to Wales that made me think, without words and in private, that I could see a clue as to how to live. The Sycamore Press especially suggested that making, knowing, and judging might be seamless. It gave an imaginative and a tangible connection to authors such as Woolf and Pope, who knew about the making or the design of books, and approached them through essentially the same technology. It gave meaning to the purely ridiculous: when my friend and fellow undergraduate Philippa and I rowed from Magdalen up to North Oxford, John waved us off from the LMH jetty with a spotted handkerchief, mopping at walrus tears – but we'd been typesetting a book that was someone's first collection, that hadn't had physical existence before, and now – incipiently – did. And the press also gave rise to something that even at the time *was* anecdote, and even at the time seemed ridiculously apt for what it said about invention and constraint: the first time Philippa and I typeset some Florio poems, including our own, John warned us that he was so short of lowercase *k* he'd made Mick Imlah rewrite a poem solely to cut down on *k*, so that it could be printed; the result, he said, was a much improved poem. It was one of those asides that stick in the mind, like the comment that syllabics don't work because they can't be heard, which came in the course of a conversation that was otherwise mostly about the Newdigate and Auden in Oxford – including, as it happens, his curtains. Of the two, though, the story about *k* seemed the more telling because the constraint it praised was more arbitrary.

At the time, all of this was both revelatory and taken for granted. Since then, though I've not really put it into words before, it's become talismanic. It's in an inner or even outer raised eyebrow when anyone mentions the business model for universities going forward or presents one too many grids in the form of forms to fill; it's in habits of bookbinding and silversmithing and writing, and in the occasional spoof footnote. Still more, it's in the surprise that any of this surprises anyone. As for summing it up... 'serious play' might cover it, though that sounds at once far too serious and slightly too flippant. It wasn't, and isn't, necessarily easy to live up to. I'm still ashamed of how very bad (and bad-tempered) I was at an elaborate form of mental Scrabble, and was floored quite recently when John asked – after a gap of months or years but as if it were part of a continuous conversation – why I don't capitalise my lines. Oh, I said, something about the counterpoint of line and sentence and a different kind of grammar... Weeks later I picked up a Florio pamphlet with long left margins of heavily indented capitals – and there at once was the reality of lead at the fingertips – the finger-nicking serif of lowercase *f* and the sensory difference between wide em-spaces and narrower en's – and with it, the sense of just beginning to see a possible way of being. So what with all the forms going forward now and the wrong sorts of grid, what I should have said – and what I then tried to say in a poem – is that capitalisation is Edenic. Though, as I was sternly but truthfully told, the poem still doesn't answer the question:

When all poems' lines began with capital initials
Houses had roots that ran down into the ground.
The rooms of the houses were the mind's interiors
Whose fingers walked them like a compositor's
Seeing feelingly the type tray's upper and lower
Orders, separating *h* from *o* and murmuring
Over the dark matter of the open spaces: *mmmn*.

When all poems' lines began with capital initials
There were no orphans and widow was erratum
For window, or windows: square, self-justifying,
Perfectly aligned. Each showed a landscape
And its familiars of off-white house, cliff,
Estuary: the mind's furniture that's configured
And reconfigured each time the poet who inhabits

The A-framed attic of the house with its view
Of a dinghy bravely bent on the horizon writes
A poem whose lines all begin with capital initials
And each initial forms an aperture on a world
In miniature whose immaculate gilt sun
Illuminates the house, the boat, the open spaces
Of the ocean O without end before the fall.

John Fuller: A Tribute*

ELISE PASCHEN

I HAD ADMIRED the poetry and the critical work of John Fuller and, when I arrived at Magdalen College in the autumn of 1982, I looked forward to studying with him. At Magdalen, I soon discovered that John also was the publisher of the Sycamore Press, and that he had published chapbooks of some of my favourite poets, including James Fenton and Andrew Motion. Sycamore Press had just produced Mick Imlah's *The Zoologist's Bath and Other Adventures*, a poetry collection which made an impact on us all.

During that first year of my M.Phil. course I studied the poetry of W. H. Auden with John, and once a week we would meet in his rooms at the New Building to discuss Auden's work. At that time John invited me to join the Florio Society, a group of Magdalen writers who gathered together to discuss each other's poems. If anyone became too self-congratulatory, Bernard O'Donoghue, a Florio Society member, would tease, 'More power to your elbow.' John urged us to work on our poems, and at Magdalen College he created a close-knit community of poets and poetry lovers.

In the spring of 1983, John encouraged Mick Imlah, Nicholas Jenkins, Nicola Richards and me to launch the literary magazine *Oxford Poetry*. Since that time, he has navigated the journal through a succession of editors. When we served as co-editors, John showed us how to edit a magazine, even driving us around London to help distribute the journals to book stores.

Some time in 1984 (I had completed my M.Phil. degree and had begun writing a D. Phil. dissertation on W. B. Yeats's manuscripts), John offered to publish my work with Sycamore Press. Some of the poems he selected, such as 'Oklahoma Home' and 'The Front Room', were ones I had written as an undergraduate at Harvard. John also included new work, such as 'On a Plane Flying Down the Coast of Florida' and 'Bluebells'. Although he was less inclined to critique individual poems, John organised the arrangement of the manuscript.

I was drawn toward the title *Landfall* for the chapbook, but a poetry book by that name had just been published in America, so we chose a new one. John pointed out that there were many images of houses in the poems as well as poems containing sea imagery. He suggested the title *Houses: Coasts*. We spent some time discussing the punctuation (*Houses, Coasts*, for instance), but then made the daring decision to use a colon. We also deliberated about the colours for the cover. The combination of sky blue and chocolate brown remains a favourite. We decided to use artwork by David Kuhn, a college friend, who had created engravings originally inspired by Seamus Heaney's 'Bog' poems. Nick Jenkins wrote the biographical copy for the pamphlet, and Nick and John did the typesetting.

During my five years at Magdalen, we spent many Saturday afternoons at John and Prue's house on Benson Place, working on various Sycamore Press pamphlets. I learned how to hand-set type. John bound the pamphlets with a needle and thread. John and Nick, during typesetting breaks, would play chess. John is also a remarkable cook, and he and Prue created delectable lunches – a smorgasbord of delicacies – from different exotic cuisines. I sampled my first Manhattan there! Their garden seemed tropical, blooming with various plants and flowers, and their cat, whose name I've forgotten, was an indomitable presence. Throughout the years various poets would help at the Press, including Bernard O'Donoghue and Mark Wormald, as well as Emily – John and Prue's youngest daughter.

John was an incredible mentor and editor. He championed and supported our poetry, from encouraging us to write new poems for the Florio Society to editing and publishing our work. He was brilliant and funny, generous and kind. I was honoured to be counted among the poets John chose to publish and privileged to be included in his company.

* First published in *John Fuller & the Sycamore Press*, ed. Ryan Roberts (Bodleian Library, 2010).

An Apology

JONATHAN KEATES

DEAR SIR,

I'm writing to apologise for not having sent you a contribution to the John Fuller festschrift.

The fact is that I feel I don't have anything original to say or an original way of expressing what I should like to say, which is that while I was an undergraduate he was an outstanding encourager and enabler of my early writing, that he and his family became my friends and that he has remained somebody for whom, in whatever sense, I always write, whose ear connects with my voice and with whose particular sense of humour I engage in my head as I write.

It's impossible for me to express what I feel about John and how much I admire what he does. His versatility and originality as a poet seem to me massively under-appreciated. Don't people know what a stupendous artist this is, for Christ's sake? He has poetry under his fingernails, at the roots of his hair, in the marrow of his bones.

I wish I had some means of saying what it is that he has meant to me since he was first my tutor at Magdalen – would I have read Gay's 'The Shepherd's Week', Garth's 'The Dispensary' or Young's 'Night Thoughts' without him, I wonder? – and then as doyen of the Florio Society, not to speak of our annual trio-sonata-playing sessions at Christmas with Sophie, Louisa and Emily. Part of everything I do as a writer is inflected by him.

But I just can't put this into any form worthy of inclusion in your collection. It's because I don't know how exactly his influence on me has worked, and yet I know that it has, acting as a benign, numinous presence throughout my creative life.

I'm terribly sorry but I just don't know how to do this successfully. You can imagine how ashamed I shall feel for being absent from among the contributors.

Sincere apologies and best wishes,
Jonathan Keates

John Fuller & the John Florio Society

ADAM THORPE

WHEN IT WAS CONFIRMED that I would take the Oxbridge exam, my English teacher, Andrew Davis, decided I should try for Magdalen College, Oxford. 'The first-year tutor is a poet, John Fuller. Perfect for you. And he's an Auden specialist as well as keen on the Augustans.' I had secretly found Auden too knotty, and we had concentrated on Pope and Johnson for what felt like much of the year: what thrilled me was that Andrew had noticed I wrote poetry.

The thought of the Oxbridge interview terrified me. Published poets occupied some unimaginable higher realm where Keats presided with his blood-spotted shirt, the living and the dead indistinguishable from one another. Among others, Lowell, Plath and Hughes were my contemporary demi-gods, joined by Geoffrey Hill through my chance discovery of *Mercian Hymns* in the school library, a volume I can confidently say changed my life – or the part of it dedicated to writing.

Living in far-off Cameroon between terms, I had very little access to books beyond those in the school and in the shops in town, and these were pre-Internet days. John Fuller's *The Mountain in the Sea* had only just been published, and I hadn't seen it, although *Epistles to Several Persons* was on the Memorial Library's shelves. I may have come across his poem 'The Cook's Lesson' in an anthology, but its opening line made a deep impression: 'When the king at last could not manage another erection...' Such a deep impression, in fact, that it was echoing in my head when I entered the room in Magdalen's New Buildings for my interview, jelly-legged and nauseous. Raised on a dais, ranged behind a large mahogany desk, the panel gazed upon me with what I interpreted as august contempt: Emrys Jones posed a few questions on Shakespeare, which I answered haltingly. Then John Fuller asked me what contemporary British poets I liked. I mentally looked around me: they had all fled, utterly disloyal – even Hill, even Hughes, even the late David Jones. My mind was scorched earth. With one exception. 'Sylvia Plath,' I stammered. 'She's American,' came the retort. I squeezed my eyes shut, temporarily the most stupid person on the planet.

The only other name that had survived this mental paralysis belonged, of course, to my interrogator. I genuinely liked what I had read of his poetry. Dismayingly, that opening line 'When the king at last could not manage another erection' was repeating itself at considerable inner volume. I could have talked about this quote: how much information, how much scene-setting, how much humour was packed into that single sentence. How the 'when' anticipated a narrative, how the 'at last' suggested a whole history beforehand (I had no technical terms for these phenomena, except for *in medias res*), as well as a speaker's voice and point of view – bureaucratically formal but weary. I could have mentioned the importance of the word 'manage' – swaying between 'achieve' and 'control'. I saw the king as flustered, fussing over his failure, although I had no idea what his excited state might have been due to or purposed for: there were no women or boys present (the king, to my mind, was a Nero figure). All this I could have discoursed on for some time, but I was paralysed by the impropriety of it: the startlingly blue eyes of the author himself were gazing down on me.

Having so dismally failed in an area that should have posed no challenge, I had no stomach for the questions on T. S. Eliot, whose poems I thought I knew well. 'Why,' asked Fuller, 'does Prufrock not dare to eat a peach?' I looked confused. I had no hope, by now, of entering Oxford. 'I mean, why a peach', he went on patiently, 'and not an apple?' Cursing myself for not ever having posed this question before, I blushingly concocted some airy nonsense about sexual symbolism and ancient myth (pomegranates and so on), and the power of the concrete image. I was interrupted mid-twaddle: 'Have you ever eaten a peach yourself?' Faintly surprised, I nodded. Fuller went on: 'It's not easy, it dribbles down your chin, it's awkward and embarrassing in public. Dare one take a bite?' I nodded gamely, but in a flash I realised the importance of cutting through intellectual bluster to the simple, straightforward quick of it. (Unfortunately, when I tentatively entered academia myself in the mid-1980s, the murky waters of its arch blusterers, the two Jacques – Lacan and Derrida – were rising fast, and I fled soon after.)

Although I learnt much later that this oral shambles cost me a scholarship, I was accepted. Fuller was much gentler in tutorials. After a term or so, I dared to show him some mini-stories published in one of the university's literary magazines. He returned them with a single comment attached with a pin, written in his characteristic brown ink and beautifully rounded hand: 'I was envious!' No critical comment since has ever made such an impact on me. At that moment I knew I could be a writer.

Just last year, feeling even less confident than I had four decades ago in these times of Amazon-starred demagoguery (semi-literates able to saw through years of intricate work in front of a global audience), I sent John the typescript of my new novel, which had just been rejected outright by both editor and agent, no redrafting permitted. He read the lot in three days flat, and replied with a letter of several pages. Not only was he highly encouraging – 'A rich book of range and depth' – but suggested why it had been rejected, and how I might resolve the impasse, short of leaving my publisher. I was eventually allowed to rework it and the novel is to be published in June 2017. 'Yes, no towels must ever be thrown in,' as he put it in an email, when I told him the good news. 'So we need to be old bruisers giving each other pep-talks before the next round!'

Back in 1977, recognising that I was obsessively writing poems, he invited me to join the John Florio Society. I had no idea who Florio was, apart from his Magdalen connection as a college tutor, and knew little more at that stage about Michel de Montaigne, whom Florio had introduced to Elizabethan England via his exquisite translation. The idea was ingeniously simple: you brought along a new poem, typed out to preserve anonymity, and added it to the pool. Someone else then read it aloud and judgement – or at least a critical debate – followed. No one must ever know which of the assembled wrote it. Among the fellow undergraduates and graduates regularly present (aside from my old school friend Christopher Edwards) were Alan Hollinghurst, Mick Imlah, Pico Iyer, David Profumo and another youngish tutor, Bernard O'Donoghue. None of us was yet published, of course. It was nerve-wracking and exciting in equal measure. By now I had found *The Mountain in the Sea* in one of the three excellent small bookshops in Newbury, where my parents had returned to from Africa, and fallen hopelessly for John's poetry. This was a genuine passion which has not diminished in forty years, and had little to do with his position as my tutor. His poetry remains one of my creative touchstones.

When the late Mick Imlah was Society secretary, the Florio meetings took place in his rooms opposite the College library in Longwall Quad. These are the gatherings I recall most clearly: a large, very soft sofa we would hope to sink into, the odd hard chair, latecomers using the rug. The experience could be frustrating: waiting heart-in-mouth for your scribble to be chosen, read (often badly), then judged. Now and again we set ourselves metrical challenges: Christopher remembers triplets in the metre of Tennyson's *Locksley Hall*, but this was an exercise which only John relished.

One of my poems featured the word 'junket' in an ambiguous role. A discussion took place. For some reason, the word was regarded as faintly amusing, but the poem itself (I forget its subject) was deadly serious. I meant it in the sense of 'jaunt'. 'Jaunt' would have been better, but at the time I favoured the obscure. Alan Hollinghurst, with his deep-voiced urbanity in which every sentence sounded expertly carved (he was my excellent post-grad tutor, though not much older than myself), told us that his mother made junkets, that it was a sort of milk pudding and quite, quite delicious. It just about worked in the context, too, although in a comic way. I was bursting with indignation during the chat about puddings that followed, but had to chuckle along with the rest. I had never heard of a junket as pudding. One's enforced silence had to endure cruel (if quite unmalicious) misreadings, of which this was a very slight example, but at least, in those days, the forums were contained within four walls. All this, of course, was highly instructive, assuming meaning was important to you as a poet.

It could work the other way, too. The best session for me was when a poem about my mother and grandmother enduring the Blitz (direct hit on the house next door) was considered to be one of John's. The Florio permitted this guesswork, but you weren't supposed to confirm or deny. They particularly liked the image of dust on the leaves of an aspidistra being gently carried out of the rubble. 'Well done, John, very good.' The assumed author simply raised his eyebrows enigmatically. I sat on the rug, scarcely able to keep quiet. It was the last poem. We rose to go. John winked at me. How did he know? I walked out into the wintry quad on air and I have never quite scraped ground since.

Fun & True

R O B E R T   S E L B Y

AS A RESEARCHER of one of his protégés, I encountered John Fuller's considerable generosity first vicariously, then directly. I first met John in the autumn of 2012 to discuss the subject of my PhD thesis, his former student and late friend Mick Imlah. The information he kindly provided formed the backbone of my doctoral essay – as it does this piece, for John's transformative effect on Imlah's poetry career is doubtless emblematic of the impact he has had on many budding young writers going back half a century.

On Tuesday 9 December 1975, the nineteen-year-old Mick Imlah attended his Oxford entrance interview; on the panel was thirty-eight-year-old Magdalen fellow and tutor John Fuller, who found the Dulwich schoolboy shy but nonetheless exuding the dexterous intellect evident in his entrance papers. Imlah was duly awarded a Demyship to study English at Magdalen, and the following autumn, in his first year, John was his tutor for Victorians and Moderns. While re-reading the poetry of Robert Browning in order to teach it on this course, John had, he told me when we met, 'suddenly myself seen all of Browning's poetry as a kind of model for the sort of thing we should be doing now: no longer the rapt lyric, but something more fictive, more teasing'. John had outlined what he meant by this in a 1989 pamphlet of Chatto poets:

I've always believed that poetry is better when it is entertainment rather than rapt self-communion, and my metaphor for that entertainment is Palace of Varieties rather than Grand Opera. I would prefer poems to be fantastic, riddling, horrific, erotic, or plain fun, rather than 'true'. The truth of poetry is a function of the reader's pleasure. (*Chatto Poetry Festival: New Statesman Contemporary Writing* No.1, 1989)

Much of John's own poetry at the time was characterised thematically by this enjoyment of the fictive and formally by the rejection of free verse. Imlah was already predisposed to these attributes, disliking, as he later told *Oxford Poetry*, poetry that could be construed as a 'coded version of the poet's life' and which on the page 'looks like rubble'. This meeting of like minds, then, made it inevitable that Imlah would join John at Magdalen's Florio Society, the venerable critical discussion group revived by John and others in 1968 after an eight-year hiatus.

The first Society meeting Imlah attended, that of Michaelmas term 1977, was in fact held in his own rooms in Magdalen's Longwall Quad; in attendance were, among others, John, College Lecturer Bernard O'Donoghue, and Junior College Lecturer Alan Hollinghurst. This was the start of a longstanding editorial friendship between Imlah and John; Imlah would, for example, send via postcard different versions of a line of poetry and, John told me,

I suppose I would always say which I preferred, and that was the kind of thing that would go on in the Florio Society. We tore into people's poems anonymously when they turned up. It was a very good way of learning from the obtuseness of the assembled company which lines work and which lines don't. So you could take that away with you as an admonitory lesson without feeling ashamed because no one knew it was your poem – except that we all did!

Even more helpful for Imlah's development as a poet was the Sycamore Press, established by John in 1968 and operating out of his spare garage in Oxford's Benson Place. For the next quarter of a century, this Arab clamshell hand-set printing press, formerly used to print cricket scorecards for the University Parks, produced – in runs of two-to-three hundred – pamphlets by students and non-students whose poetry John felt deserved a wider audience: among its fruits was debut or early work by James Fenton (1968 and 1981), David Harsent (1973), Andrew Motion (1977) and Alan Hollinghurst (1982), with Imlah joining them in 1982 with his *The Zoologist's Bath and Other Adventures*. Motion has said of his Sycamore experience: 'Knowing the poems had John's blessing gave me a valuable sort of confidence.' Being published by the Sycamore Press provided not just moral support, but invaluable practical help too: for example, some of Fenton's debut pamphlet, *Our Western Furniture*, was broadcast on BBC Radio, while Imlah's pamphlet received a review by Peter Porter in the *Observer*. The Sycamore process had transformed Imlah from a promising undergraduate poet into a published poet with an audience. 'We enjoyed the printing of these things,' said John,

circulating them, publicising them. We used to go around to bookshops – six copies here in Oxford and in Compendium Books in London, six copies out to Alan Hancock's in Cheltenham and that kind of thing – and send out copies for review. With regards to reviews, if I could pull a string

I'd pull a string. I didn't have that many strings to pull, but whenever I could and I thought it was worth it and thought it might come off, I'd do it.

The tortuous process of producing pamphlets on a treadle-powered machine and typesetting by hand for as long as the daylight lasted, carried out on weekends (and aided by the poets themselves), was emblematic of Fuller's tireless generosity with his time:

I do sometimes now miss the printing; it was very primitive, very old-fashioned, and very time consuming. I don't know as a retired person now how I fitted in everything I had to do when I was younger – you know, teaching, lecturing, writing, printing, all those things. It was great fun just messing around with machines, quite apart from the feeling that you are circulating some marvellous poem that no one had read yet and will.

John thus provided an immense service for young poetry-writing students, the like of which has not been and perhaps can never be replicated by modern creative writing courses: the acceptance into a charmed world of intellectual exchange; the rigorous workshopping of one's creative work by peers and published writers; the opportunity to publish one's poetry, and one's writings on poetry, in *Oxford Poetry* (which John – who else? – was pivotal in reviving in 1983); and the possibility of publishing one's work as a pamphlet with the Sycamore Press, which could lead to national recognition. John, then, was very much what Motion has called the 'presiding genius' for successive generations of poetry-writing Oxford students.

It is indicative of the man that a number of John's students graduated from Oxford as his friend. For many years after leaving, Imlah would holiday at John's cottage on the Llŷn Peninsula. And such friendships John still cultivates: *AWOL* (Emma Press, 2015), his recent epistolary collaboration with a poet more than fifty years his junior, Magdalen alumnus and Florio Society secretary Andrew Wynn Owen, is testament to that. At *AWOL*'s London launch, John spoke about the conception of the book's verse-letter dialogue:

We at the Florio enjoyed practising verse forms which Andrew as secretary had set everybody – double ballads and sestinas and quatrains and terza rimas and goodness knows what. So it seemed entirely appropriate when term came to an end and I rather missed all this fun to write him a letter wondering where he was.

John's ostensibly light-hearted terza rima contributions in *AWOL* continue a preoccupation that has crept into his *oeuvre* in recent years: mortality. In poem nine, he laments various neighbours in Wales who have now passed away:

Neighbours, all of them, not here.
Not anywhere, if truth be told.
Neighbours are strange, neighbours are dear,

Defining how a place can hold
A special fascination for
The people in it who grow old

Together, though we know no more
Of each than gossip at the gate
Or what we glimpse through a front door.

Yes, they are gone, and it's too late
To ask them now the things I wanted
About what led them to their fate,

What childhood disappointments haunted
Them, what flags of pain ignored,
What futile hopes pursued undaunted.

As he has moved through his seventies and friends and contemporaries have begun to depart, John's poetic persona has increasingly felt as though life is – as he puts it in 'Somewhere Else' from *The Dice Cup* (Chatto, 2014) – 'a party that has gone on too long', at which those who remain are left to imagine those who've departed 'gathering somewhere else, with relieved comments about their lucky escape'. In *AWOL*, this persona plays the obstinate stay-at-home ('don't travel', he declares) to Wynn Owen's bright-eyed young traveller, because to leave one's friends for distant climes seems, now, too akin to the final departure we all must eventually undertake. In 'Dispersals', also from *The Dice Cup*, he feels more sharply the 'primal anxiety' that comes from the 'dispersal' of his loved ones ('Louisa in Lisbon, Sophie in Venice, Prue in Brazil') and contemplates whether, if heaven exists and is a good place, it is there that such dispersing is reversed:

[...] space is terrifying! There is far too much of it. And what is all this moving on but a tentative exploration, like children in a dark cellar with linked hands? When hands are held, all life is in that contact of the skin. Far from dispersing, the whole of matter is howling to be joined up. If we could unite the family, the race, the species, and reverse its atomisation, is this what a heaven might be?

If dispersal is a characteristic of life, one hopes John will have to make do with phone calls, emails and postcards for many years to come.

Since first meeting John I personally have gained a small insight into what being one of his students must have been like: he has always made himself available to help with queries regarding my thesis; taken the time to read poems of mine and commented incisively upon them; blurbed a selection of Imlah's prose that I co-edited; posted me his Christmas quiz (a poem he penned in impeccable quatrains containing 'at least seventy-four hidden words, all related in some way' – answers on a postcard, small prize for the winner); and always got in touch should he discover that I have yet again been asked to write about him ('I do believe that you have written most of the reviews that I have had in the last 18 months'). I have been lucky enough to join a large and ever-expanding body of people who have been enabled by John's generosity, and those people, like John's faithful band of readers, are filled with gladness when they read in *AWOL* that this pillar of post-war poetry in England, now moving into his ninth decade, is 'dismissing / Any idea of a vacation'.

John Fuller

ANDREW MOTION

I WENT UP TO OXFORD in 1970, and because no one on my father's side had been to university before, and my mother's family were largely unknown to me, I felt I had a lot of catching up to do. I felt nervous as well, which meant (among other things) that it took me a while to pluck up the courage to write to Roy Fuller, then Professor of Poetry, and ask to meet him. He of course agreed immediately, and suggested we had a cup of coffee at his son's house in Benson Place, in the not-very-northerly part of Oxford known as North Oxford.

This would have been in 1972, I think, and by this stage I'd read a lot of John's poems. I'd heard a lot about him, too – mainly from Alan Hollinghurst, whom I got to know around the same time and whom was quickly becoming my best friend. But I'd never actually met him. I was at University College, not John's college Magdalen, and I wasn't that keen on (or any good at) the literary quizzes that might have drawn us together elsewhere. But now there he was, looking on while I drank my coffee with Roy. I don't think we spoke much. I felt so anxious throughout the whole encounter, poring over some dreadful poems I'd sent ahead of me, I doubt that whatever I did say to either of them made much sense.

It wasn't that Roy was frightening; on the contrary, he was extremely courteous. And neither did John come across as formidable; it was more that he had a formidable reputation. As a poet, of course, then coolly associated with the very cool world of Ian Hamilton's *Review* and then *New Review*; as a critic who had found his way through the thorniest thickets of Auden's poems; and as a teacher and inspirer of poets younger than himself – most notably James Fenton, who had already left Oxford by the time Alan and I arrived, but whose spirit lingered in a way that was both exciting and intimidating.

In person, by contrast, John was... Well, as I say, I only saw him in the side of my eye, that time with his father. But when I finished my first degree in 1974 and began to do my research – on Edward Thomas – John was appointed my supervisor and moved to the centre of my life. We used to meet in his rooms in Magdalen a couple of times a term, and talk about whatever chapters or bits of chapters I'd sent him since our last encounter, then go and have lunch together in Hall. I was obsessed by Thomas – I still am – and fired by the sense (now extinguished) that he was 'unfairly neglected'. This meant I didn't need much encouragement to get on with my work. But I did need to be directed, focused, and made to think around the poems (by exploring other writers in Thomas's tradition and his time). John did all this for me and more. In particular he made me more willing than I would otherwise have been to ask unexpected questions (one about a possibly erotic element in the poem 'Old Man' I remember especially well).

Remarkably, he made all this happen without seeming to exert himself. I mean, he was obviously completely engaged with whatever we were talking about, but there was no sense of strain or busyness or push-and-shove about his interrogations. Just an easy kind of power, which combined braininess with an almost innocent-seeming curiosity. With hindsight I can see that combination is very similar to the organising principle of his poetry, where we find extraordinary technical skill (he's one of the most adroit formalists of the last century) used to release an imagination that is exceptionally daring. Not just squaring up to the difficult Big Things in boldly straightforward ways (in his wonderful elegy for Francis Hope, for instance), but delighting in oddity too, in quirkiness, even a sophisticated kind of facetiousness.

Like everyone he taught, I owe him a great deal. Not just in university ways (my thesis), and poetic ways (he printed what became the title-poem of my first book on his Sycamore Press), but in making me feel connected with contemporaries I liked and admired very much: Alan, of course, in particular, and also Mick Imlah. I wouldn't say we were a school, exactly (our styles were too diverse for that), but we took courage from one another, and from our shared admiration for John. And yet like everyone who might want to praise him in these or any other terms, I can imagine him shrugging it off, and saying something like 'I don't think I taught you anything, really.' But that modesty was an essential part of his influence, and of his genius as a person. It meant that for all his exceptional cleverness, there was no un-crossable barrier dividing him from the world. No wonder so many of his former charges have become his friends.

In my own case, I wish that circumstances had allowed friendship to flower even more broadly than it has done. I have a lot of fond memories of meetings and meals with John – and with Prue and the girls, and one especially happy recollection of a punting expedition on the Cherwell, which one of my then-young children enjoyed so much he felt compelled to prove it by throwing himself into the river. And in a different sort of way, I feel proud that Chatto became John's publishers when I worked there during the 1980s. But I also know that our separate busynesses, and our living in different cities (now over three thousand miles apart) set a kind of boundary. Not to mention my hopelessness at all things Nemo-ish (though I did do the easy thing one year, and contribute a guest page of quotations). But that's what the best teachers do, isn't it, and the best friends. They always give us the sense there's more to be learned, and more to be said. Happy birthday, dear John, and thank you.

The Making of *Dream Hunter*: A Conversation

John Fuller & Nicola LeFanu

DREAM HUNTER IS A chamber opera for four singers and chamber ensemble (seven players), with music by Nicola LeFanu and libretto by John Fuller, duration c. 55 minutes, commissioned by the Mornington Trust, premiered winter 2011.

The setting is early-twentieth-century Corsica. Men can have an active, outdoor life, while women are secluded, domestic. But some women find they are gifted with 'second sight', with the prescience of death: they are *mazzere*. In their dreams they hunt and kill – hare, deer or wild boar. Then someone in their village falls sick or dies. To have the power of the *mazzere* is a dubious honour. If they foresee death, do they also cause it?

In the dilapidated farmhouse of Domenico, a widowed small-holder, his daughters Angela and Catarina prepare the evening meal. Angela, the elder sister, hopes that tonight will confirm her betrothal to Sampiero, son of the local mayor; she is anxious to make a good impression. Catarina's thoughts are far away: last night she had a strange dream of hunting in the hills and wounding a hare. She is horrified that most of her father's land will go to Sampiero as Angela's dowry; and she has reason to know that this urbane young man is a philanderer. Sampiero has secrets of his own: a gambler, he is in debt to Domenico.

Sampiero arrives early to see the girls – a breach of convention. But Domenico returns with wild boar shot out of season, a worse transgression. As night falls, the men turn to brandy; the women are left with their troubled thoughts. When Domenico has fallen into a drunken sleep, Sampiero creeps into the girls' bedroom, seeking Catarina. But who is the predator, who the prey?

Dream Hunter uses a historical setting but it deals with issues that are alive in the present day: the confusion between reality and 'virtual' reality, the enforced seclusion of women. The following conversation was first published in the programme for the London premiere in January 2012.

John Fuller: I was thrilled when you came to me with the proposal that we write a short opera. After the dramatic monologue 'Alkman' and the love-lyrics 'The Tongue and the Heart', it seemed the next step for us to be writing an opera, didn't it?

Nicola LeFanu: I loved the Russian scenario you came up with first: it had the ideal combination of being lively and indeed funny while dealing with very serious issues. And its dramaturgy, its elegant stagecraft, appealed to me. I do hope we get the opportunity to do it! But it was too ambitious for this project, which I wanted to make just right for Lontano.

J.F. I got carried away, and it would have been a whole evening with rather complicated effects. A chamber opera, as I soon found out, is a more concentrated affair. I very much wanted a Corsican subject, and for a while thought I had found one in Merimée's story 'Matteo Falcone'. Since *Carmen* was based on Merimée, its credentials were perfect, I thought. It has suspense, betrayal, moral conflict, and best of all very few characters!

N.L. Yes, but no female characters – that's a great drawback for me as the soprano voice is the most beautiful instrument to write for and the main part would have been a treble. Britten could have done it, but I did not want to go down his path.

J.F. Yes, there's a small boy at the centre of it, who would be so difficult to cast. You'd have to go, as you say, in the direction of Miles in *The Turn of the Screw*, or Hansel in the Humperdinck, and either way looked ruinous for us. So instead I invented a story based on the tradition of the *mazzere*, the dream hunters of Corsica.

N.L. This story grabbed me – again, because it worked on several levels: a gripping story, but serious issues underneath. Although I had never been to Corsica, it seemed to me a generic European tale; rural Ireland was full of these kinds of beliefs. And though it was set in the late nineteenth century, it was dealing with issues that are topical today.

J.F. Yes, it has everything an opera should have: passion, greed, jealousy... and the supernatural! But did you find this deliberate historical setting something of a problem? It is common in opera, after all.

N.L. Well, at first I thought a 'verismo' libretto was a bit of a conundrum for a living composer! But once I got inside the text and the musical ideas began to develop, it wasn't a problem. Starting with a folksong was more challenging...

J.F. I don't mind contemporary verismo at all! Early Fellini, for example, is terrifically operatic. All those naked emotions and voluble egotism! But why was the folksong challenging?

N.L. Vernacular folksong today is so different from its nineteenth-century self. I read Caroline Bithell's superb book on Corsican music, and you had already lent me a CD of Corsican sacred music. It was not for me to appropriate any of that; but I soon realised that there was a pan-European tradition, which I'd experienced on my visits to Farrera, in the remote Catalan Pyrenees. There, a few people are still making up songs and singing them in the old ways – unaccompanied and informal. I drew on that for the simple, diatonic song for the girls; later, I discovered the extent to which it was the seed of the more complex music that follows. I thought the men needed a folksong too – to open with one and then never again would be rather odd – hence the drinking song.

J.F. Yes, you wrote the tune first and I had to fit the

words to it. That was quite a challenge. Your notes seemed to go on forever, so the words of the song have to have very long lines. But I like these challenges. Like trying to write some cod French for that fragment of quoted operetta.

N.L. I used Offenbach in the end! It was great that in our collaboration we could spark ideas back and forth in that way: it's one of the big rewards of a hybrid medium like opera. Skype helped us, didn't it?

J.F. It did. York meets Oxford at the press of a button! But I was fascinated by the whole refining process. My first detailed prose sketches had all the essential dramatic lineaments of the thing, but allowed for elements that turned out to be red herrings (was Angela also a *mazzera*, for example?). Then when we had argued about the psychology and motivation and I had drafted and re-drafted the scenario, I could get down to the business of deciding what words to use and what sort of shape they should take. I decided on short lines of verse, with plenty of largely unobtrusive rhyming. I thought that it would carry the necessary forward propulsion of the dialogue, and also help the audience to hear and predict the words.

N.L. I remember quoting Boito and Verdi to you ('music takes five times as long as words') and saying how economic the libretto had to be for a fifty-minute opera. You were so generous, you said I could cut ('slash and burn!') as much as I liked. But your poetic words were my inspiration. I cut very little, until I prevented you giving Catarina an extra aria at the end.

J.F. That happily now-truncated aria was my desire to give Catarina a sort of noble assertiveness at her moment of greatest self-understanding. It would have been all right in a verse play by Yeats, but libretti are, as you say, skinnier than verse plays.

N.L. Catarina was a marvellous character to create. Her vocal line has to show her growing up: she's hardly more than a child at the opening, but she becomes a young woman who is fully aware of her power. Her music has to embody all that; and just as she flies in her dreams, so I knew that her vocal line would fly, as it does in the finale.

J.F. Of course. And the greatest lesson the librettist learns (and re-learns!) is that finally it is the music that does everything. Your flying vocal line is also supported by techniques of musical allusion (leitmotifs, and so on) that do more complicated work than the often unheard words can do.

N.L. I think the most important job the music has to do, alongside the characterisation, is pace the drama. Pacing is all! And yes, a wide range of musical techniques come into play, but I like them to be hidden; the listener does not need to know that an aria is tightly made because it is a canon, or whatever. Which bit of the libretto did you enjoy writing most? Do you have a favourite bit of text?

J.F. Very hard to say, not least because the librettist

should beware of having favourite bits. It will probably mean that instead of serving the composer's needs, as he should do, he has gone off on some verbal ego-trip. But I did like trying to give Catarina's hunting dream at the end a sexual edge that would counterbalance her otherwise innocent or chaste reserve. She has to terrify Sampiero at this point and put his shallow opportunistic lewdness to shame. I also liked the purely non-verbal aspect of writing the libretto, arranging the pace and condensation of the story, and trying to maintain the dramatic tension. I enjoyed creating the structural and visual parallel between the dead boar and corpse of Sampiero, for example (though it proves tricky in production). It is just the right sort of element that creates a meaning quite outside mere words. What about you? What part of the composition engaged you most?

N.L. Certainly Catarina's part and her arias, but I think perhaps even more so Angela's aria. Your words released something special. And I realised then that Angela had to be a mezzo, not a contralto as I'd thought, because she is so vulnerable. The low range of soprano, mezzo and contralto all have tellingly different colours, though the notes may look the same.

J.F. Your setting of Angela's aria is so beautiful. It surprised me into realising that its sentiments are somehow at the heart of the opera (just as it chances to come at the very midpoint of the score). I hadn't really foreseen that. But there are always surprises, not least in what emerges in an actual production. Take Sampiero, for example. As I conceived him, he is not much more than a shabby provincial dandy who would be (has been!) an utter failure as a womaniser, despite his knowingness and bravado. The failed magic trick indicates this, though it is otherwise interpreted by Catarina. In production, Sampiero can come across quite differently.

N.L. From a nineteenth-century standpoint, Domenico and Sampiero behave in conventional ways, ways that would have been found acceptable. The girls love their father, and Angela clearly loves Sampiero; and so we have some sympathy for these men – the *dénouement* is their tragedy too, not just Angela's. But if the men (Sampiero especially) are interpreted in a modern way, then they lose our sympathy. The opera is intentionally ambiguous in this, I think. I am glad, too, that we have left the ending ambiguous as to what lies ahead for Catarina. For myself, I think that she is going to be a survivor.

J.F. That seems to be her immediate resolve, certainly. How, though, is a problem. It is likely that in reality she would become an object of fear and suspicion in the village, and that after her father's eventual demise no one would dare go near her. She might turn into a tough old goat woman in leather breeches, with a shotgun! It might well be Angela who would get her unexpected second chance after all. But as you say, we have engineered a quite different future for Catarina, one which happily exists only in the collective speculation of the audience, and in the abstract suggestions of the music.

John Fuller in Early Autumn

NEIL POWELL

WHAT GOT ME writing poetry, I've sometimes said, was the first edition of Alvarez's anthology *The New Poetry*, the one with the raspberry-and-grey amoeba-patterned cover in those friendly old Penguin Poets; it was published in the spring of 1962, just after my fourteenth birthday. And I'd add that its most urgent prompting came from the poems of Thom Gunn, which were unlike anything I'd previously read. But I was forgetting something else about that book. At the end, very much as a coda, were five sonnets by a poet several years younger than anyone else in *The New Poetry*: 'John Fuller (b. 1937) is doing research at New College, Oxford, where he won the Newdigate Prize in 1960.' His first collection, *Fairground Music*, was already published, but too recently to make the biographical note. 'Wow,' I thought, 'he's still a student and already in a Penguin anthology! I'd better set to work.' John Fuller had embarked, sooner than he might have guessed, on his lifetime of encouraging younger writers.

Like his father Roy Fuller, who published his first collection in 1939 and so wasn't quite a 'thirties' poet, John found himself between readily identifiable literary movements: a good place to be in terms of creative independence, if less helpful for easy reputation-building. Those early sonnets hint at other similarities between father and son: a lifelong interest in poetic forms and extended sequences; a shared admiration of Auden, on whose work John would in due course publish a magisterial commentary; a tendency to seem personally reticent or even elusive, quite unlike the 'confessional' poets of the 1960s. These are qualities which set him apart from the *Review* group of writers – especially from the jagged, intense little poems of Ian Hamilton – with whom he was perhaps associated more by intellectual rigour and Oxonian proximity than by literary temperament. And even in his early poems there's already that relish of the ludic which befits the future compiler of *Nemo's Almanack* and author of *Who Is Ozymamdias?* He is, among other things, a poetic Araucaria.

Whereas more restless poets, rashly ignoring Larkin's insistence that 'It's not the place's fault', switch careers and move house, John Fuller – once again, like his father – has stayed put. Immediately after the war, Roy resumed his job with the Woolwich, settled in Blackheath, and from then on didn't budge; John has been a fellow of Magdalen, living in the same North Oxford home, since 1966. I think it's reasonable to suggest that, in each case, sustained literary productivity has been greatly assisted by a wise refusal to faff about with pointlessly time-wasting upheavals. Both father and son (one more comparison) are authors of dauntingly extensive poetic *oeuvres*, from which it's difficult to select: with some poets, it becomes dismayingly easy to name the half-dozen greatest hits, recurrent anthology pieces, but with both Fullers you have to take the books down from the shelves and re-explore. The effect is engrossing and can be chastening: I was struck by the way in which work from different periods of John's career, stored in the depths of my ramshackle memory, was quickly nudged back to the surface. I've been particularly drawn to a pair of recurring thematic strands: those poems which take his retreat in Wales as their starting-point – among them, his 1975 collection *The Mountain and the Sea* and the long closing poem in *The Grey and the Green* (1988) – and those which engage, always perceptively, with music. He may yet make a Brahmsian of me.

Just as striking (and a special pleasure to report on this occasion) is the way in which so many of his strengths are distilled in his most recent collection, *Gravel in My Shoe* (2015). The style, pared-down yet inventive as ever, both lucid and ludic, now seems to comprehend most of English poetry. For instance: 'Here in the mind's enclosed retreat' might be a line from Marvell; 'It is like that stretch of cold brown tide / And its quivering foam on a windy day' could be Hardy; while 'My eye follows itself until / A line has been created out of air. / It wanders through the areas it defines [...]' sounds like Gunn at his most ruminative; and so on. But they are all John Fuller; all precisely right in the poems that contain them. And although *Gravel in My Shoe* is inescapably a book about getting older, it's neither finicky nor complaining; instead, it ruefully celebrates the absurdity and the resilience of the human animal. Alongside the lyrics are three extended pieces. One is 'spoken' by Mary Price (1869–1944), a solitary Welsh woodswoman; the others are, characteristically, a verse letter and a sonnet sequence. Both of them find wonderfully apt musical terms for the process of ageing. In 'The Pigeons', John describes 'these lazy years / That once I named the "antepenultimate"' (his father would have liked that word) as follows:

They're like a cadenza in the final movement
That takes material from the opening theme
And turns it over, looking for improvement,
Ruminative, wistful, like a dream
Of something to be perfected, that might seem
At last worthy of having been proposed,
A case to be considered, not yet closed.

And in 'Sketches from the Sierra de Tejeda', a cool autumnal morning suddenly prompts him to recall the 'sweet riff' of Stan Getz's solo in 'Early Autumn': 'Music contains you and the time you heard it. / Sixty years, the difference between / The music in the air and in your head.' Early autumn, with plenty of time still to go, seems the right season to come at the end of *Gravel in My Shoe*.

I was lucky enough to meet Roy Fuller in 1970 and, twenty years later, to write a book about him; John, surely to no one's surprise, was as unfailingly helpful and generous as his father had been to me. So even if, as a non-Oxonian, I've a sense of not quite belonging at this party, that bothers me not at all: I'm reminded of my favourite character in Beatrix Potter, the toad Mr Jackson, whom the house-proud Mrs Tittlemouse won't have at *her* party on account of his wet feet. Instead, he sits outside in the sun, sipping an acorn-cup of honey-dew and remarking, very sagely as it seems to me, 'Tiddly, widdly, widdly! Your very good health, Mrs Tittlemouse!' And yours too, Mr Fuller!

A Blue Array

Anne Carson, *Float*
Jonathan Cape, 2016 (£16.99)

Reviewed by JAY DEGENHARDT

A TRANSPARENT plastic box encloses Anne Carson's *Float*, a stack of twenty-two chapbooks. One side of the container is missing, through which the assorted poems, lectures, essays, and performances fall out. The contents page comes towards the top of this stack, and the works are listed in alphabetical order. By the time the collection fell into my hands, this order was gone – if it had ever been there to begin with. There is something more than aleatory in the composition, the swirling and perforated pile that practically encourages readers to lose any coherent arrangement they establish between the texts, ranging from discourse on the translation of silence to an elegy for a brother encoded in an elegy for a sister-in-law. The entire point seems to be more the absence of an established order – any established order – than the reader's choice in creating one. There is one exception to the provisional alphabetism of the contents page; at its centre lies '108 (*flotage*)', a poem in the form of a list from 1 to 108. Rather than being a stable island upon which the rest of the collection can settle, we find it is punctured throughout by skipped or lost articles, 'like a winter sky, high, thin, restless, unfulfilled. That's when I started to think about the word *flotage*.'

The booklets themselves have sleek, delicate pages; the paper covers range from pale green to deepest ocean blue, like the view one has of the spectrum of light filtered by water, fading into navy as one sinks from the surface of the sea, or the growing of light into a brilliant viridian as one floats up out of the depths. Or it is none of these, arranged – as it was for me – without colour-coding, a splash of contrasting hues as if the reader is floating face-up along a turbulent river, submerged at some moments, at others dazzled by the blinding gold of the sun. And this is true to the experience of reading this vertiginous array of texts. The excruciating fragility of the chapbooks gives the impression that they intend to get damaged, or lost, to show up in streets and garbage piles like the torn papyrus manuscripts of Sappho (translated by Carson in her faithful yet innovative book *If Not, Winter* (2002)). Where translation becomes exciting for Carson is at the 'drenched layers of nothing' it encounters, knowledge untold and works destroyed, all allowing us to feel 'that something has passed us and kept going, that some possibility has got free'. The chapbooks are, in both senses, unbound; and there is a powerful sense of freedom and movement in the frail evanescence of these loose papers cradled inside their open box. Carson has long been interested in translation, whether of language, style, or form; its indeterminacy seems the key to her means of making things new. Her latest work is no exception: many of the pieces were originally performances or lectures, translated now into poetry. No part of it is not restless, not unfulfilled in some way that leaves it untranslatable, exhilarating.

It's easy to imagine the scraps themselves floating downstream, down streams of owners and borrowers and bins and pockets, and along the ripples they are sure to leave in the literary world, the pages tearing and staining as they go, transforming into fragments and fragments of fragments. They certainly float into the collection as easily as they promise to flow apart from one another: there is little consistency in their origins – some are old, some new. 'What is the future doing underneath the past? asks Carson in 'Cassandra Float Can', 'And how does it alter you to see it there floating and how can it float?' This is buoyant writing that rises up from within the reader as well as without, in feelings of pathos, hope, nausea, and laughter.

'Powerless Structures Fig. II (Sanne)' manages all of these – a strange, meandering piece that memorialises the death of Carson's brother, describing its impact upon his wife. The focus has a dolly-zoom effect, at once myopic in detail and sweeping in vision, the poem's voice both near and far. There is a detachment in her descriptions of her widowed sister-in-law, mediated by the long-distance phone call at the centre of the poem, where the speaker hears of her brother's death: 'what's that / sound the dog oh you have a dog yes we have a dog no *I* have a dog'. This same distancing is what makes the poem haunting – the withdrawal from the source of the speaker's grief, always told slant, or water-warped by tears.

The answer to cliché, Carson writes, is 'catastrophe'. In 'Variations on the Right to Remain Silent', she describes this as the evasiveness of Joan of Arc refusing to describe the voice of God in her trial, 'the presence of a sentence that stops itself', the arrival of words that remain untranslatable. In the sixteenth century women were thrown into rivers, named witches if they managed to float. Anne Carson is with Joan of Arc on the burning stake, with the torn fragments of Sappho. She has created a text that will survive in its destruction. She floats.

An Intercourse with Ghosts

Jonathan Ellis (ed), *Letter Writing Among Poets: From William Wordsworth to Elizabeth Bishop*
Edinburgh University Press, 2016

Reviewed by RUTH HAWTHORN

THE DEMISE OF LETTER WRITING has been pronounced prematurely on numerous occasions over the last two centuries; the penny post, telegrams and telephones were all wrongly accused of sounding its death knell. More recently the internet and the ephemeral communication it facilitates has been decried as the final proverbial nail. As one commentator mourns, 'Inky manuscripts contain insights that can be lost forever to the backspace key.' While letters may not yet be completely extinct, as Jonathan Ellis observes, 'However one dates the "great age of letter-writing" there seems little doubt that it is in the past.' Ending, appropriately, with Ellis's own haunting essay about the last letters of John Keats, Elizabeth Bishop and Ted Hughes, *Letter Writing Among Poets* reads as an elegy for the form. What emerges in many of the essays collected here is a sense of letters' uncanniness, and Kafka's view of letters as 'an intercourse with ghosts' permeates the collection. The absent presence of the letter-writing voice (analogous with the lyric voice) and letters' ability to vividly recall the voice of the dead is commonly remarked upon, but, Ellis observes, this also works the other way: the addressee 'is ghostly too'. The necessary lag between writing and reading means that, as Angela Leighton suggests, 'there is a potential dead letter at the heart of every missive'.

There is some speculation on new media and how the role of letters is being supplanted or transformed in the age of near-instantaneous correspondence. Hermione Lee comments, for example, that 'No-one yet knows how far the ephemeral data of emails, texts, blogs and tweets will be available to the life-writers of the next centuries', while Ellis mentions rapidly changing technologies of communication and Daniel Karlin touches on the 'seductive potential of electronic editions' for literary scholars. However, these considerations are brief and, for the most part, the collection looks backwards rather than forwards, celebrating the productive hybridity of letters as 'not only a source of information but a form of information'; letters are taken seriously as an art form in their own right, rather than a secondary source the critic mines for insights. Central to the collection is the shared conviction that letters are not 'autobiography by another name' but rather 'performances' and that 'Poets are particularly adept at exploiting the letter form's bordering, edge-like nature and incorporating these discoveries in their poetry.'

Covering the Romantic period through to the twentieth century, the volume addresses a miscellany of subjects, although Keats and Bishop are, rightly, important touchstones throughout. From Anne Fadiman's reclamation of Hartley Coleridge, to Frances Wilson's chapter on the Wordsworths' love letters and Matthew Campbell's account of the mystic correspondence between George and William Butler Yeats, the essays are penetrating and engagingly written. The book is divided into three parts, beginning with a series of essays discussing broad themes and contexts, followed by chronological sections on Romantic, Victorian, and twentieth-century letters. The first section comprises Lee's thoughts on the challenges of using letters as biographical sources; Karlin's essay on editing poems within letters, which uses Keats' 'Why did I laugh tonight' as a case study; an anecdotal piece by Thomas Travisano on his experience of editing the Bishop-Lowell correspondence; and Hugh Haughton's chapter on 'the poetics of the letter'.

The concerns addressed in this first section are picked up and reconsidered throughout the rest of the volume. For instance, Travisano's experience of being barred, on Bishop's request, from reading her letters to Moore at the Rosenbach archive – although he had 'already found the material [he] most needed' – raises the uncomfortable dilemma of accessing and using personal correspondence, potentially against the writer's explicit wishes. (This is something Lee also touches on in her discussion of Tennyson's famous admonishment of those who use letters to 'make you utter things you did not say'.) The critics in this collection do not rehash ethical controversies, but instead read the tension between public and private, which comes to the fore particularly in consciously literary letters, as a potentially fertile one. Siobhan Phillips, in her excellent essay on the epistolary poetics of Lorine Niedecker, argues that Niedecker 'worked consistently [against her mentor Louis Zukofsky's modernist dictates] to make the "small circle" of correspondence coincide with the "vaguer public" of poetry'. Madeline Callaghan makes similar observations in her equally perceptive piece on Percy Shelley's verse epistles: 'These categories shift and blur as the letters become addressed to posterity and the poetry addressed to his intimate acquaintances.' Both Phillips and Callaghan also share Karlin's and Haughton's insistence that poems and letters are symbiotic, a contention Angela Leighton explores further in her chapter on W. S. Graham: 'The letter may be the place where the poem takes shape, where lines of poetry emerge from the prose, where talking to another becomes talking to oneself, and therefore where distinctions break down.' The close relationship between poems and letters is perhaps taken to its limit in Muldoon's lively essay which explores Bishop and Lowell's thirty-year exchange. While I fall among the readers Muldoon predicts will accuse him of over-reading, 'exaggerating the nasty subtext' between the pair, it is undeniable that their letters and poems constitute a densely intertextual web of reciprocal influence and shared images.

Letter Writing among Poets joins a growing body of texts devoted to the form, such as John O'Connell's eulogy *For the Love of Letters* (2012), Liz Williams' popular history *Kind Regards: The Lost Art of Letter Writing* (2012) and *The Gorgeous Nothings* (2013), which offers us facsimiles of Emily Dickinson's envelope manuscripts. This suggests that as letter writing fades from general use, it is becoming an ever more popular subject of study. Ellis's collection is a more scholarly addition, but it is an equally compelling read; as the field continues to develop, we can hope for more work of this calibre.

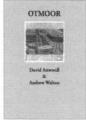

Impressions

Claire Crowther, *Bare George*, Shearsman, £6.50 • Carrie Etter, *Scar*, Shearsman, £6.50 • Helen Tookey, *In the Glasshouse*, Happen*Stance*, £5 • David Wilson, *Slope*, smith/doorstop, £5 • Mark Hinchliffe, *The Raven and the Laughing Head*, Calder Valley, £7 • David Attwooll (poems) & Andrew Walton (drawings), *Otmoor*, Black Poplar, £6 • Geraldine Clarkson, *Declare*, Shearsman, £6.50

Reviewed by ALISON BRACKENBURY

MANY OF US, harassed, screen-gazing, fail to be impressed by the sheer oddness of our world. Not Claire Crowther. Poet in residence at the Royal Mint Museum, she considers a George III sovereign. Above his rearing horse and 'crumpled' dragon, she sees an almost naked man: the Bare George of her pamphlet's title.

Unlike the coin, Crowther is not straightforwardly impressed by the Saint:

That's not
my story of men:

       The skin moves on his muscle, sun
       over down land

The authority of the poem's voice and the beauty of its vowels create a different currency. Crowther's writing has a riddling intensity, as in a poem based on another George (Herbert): 'Oh but the cost a loss of made things makes.' Her rhymes' urgent music stays new-minted: '*In hurt country / you cane the dark with rain*'. 'Come down, soft metal'. Crowther's poems honour industrially 'made things', with her own stamp: 'the furnace / that I say is famous for women's work'. Though they keep pace with the Mint's '*one thousand blanks a minute*', her poems scrutinise the tooling for a warrior's image: the 'die, the bullet-headed punch'. Reviewers can rarely generalise about the impact made by a poet's words. But at readings I have seen audience members, whose own words are very different, throng to buy Crowther's work, deeply impressed by her condensed, quick-witted poems.

🖎 Carrie Etter's *Scar* is described by her publisher as a single poem, fluid as Crowther's soft metal, exploring 'effects of climate change on her home state of Illinois'. Each observation has a whole page. This generosity, ideal for a pamphlet, is put to impressive use by Etter. Her account of a White House fact-sheet ends with unabashed lyricism: 'O Illinois –'.

The passion of *Scar* is political. It has huge shifts of scale, as a tornado hurls

             a child's treehouse

its scar in the earth visible

          from space

Links of meaning leap across pages, as climate affects 'Illinois [...] Egypt'. But Etter includes her land's own voices. 'It's a wonder we aren't all alcoholics', a farmer comments after '30 inches of rain'.

Although strikingly well informed, Etter makes fearless excursions into feeling: 'and a helicopter – with such snow, such winds – / cannot deliver the heart // in time'. *Scar*'s ending is starkly focused. Its speaker is declared 'the world's curse'– for the poem's compassionate, musical voice is human.

'This is the century in which man can determine the planet's future' (Professor Martin Rees, at the *Nature Matters* conference, Cambridge, 22 September 2016). I was impressed by his calm, scientific wisdom. I am equally impressed that, in *Scar*, Carrie Etter offers both a view from space and reflections on our troubled planet's smallest residents: 'am I [...] the field mouse scrabbling / in grain-rich dirt...'?

🖎 Reviewers, like politicians, should declare interests. Before considering Helen Tookey's Happen*Stance* chapbook, I will declare that, in 2018, I hope to have a Happen*Stance* chapbook, based on the handwritten recipes from my grandmother's years as an Edwardian cook. This has no link to my lesser labours in prose. During my decade as a reviewer, editors have let me loose on remarkably few Happen*Stance* poets. I hope that quotations from *In the Glasshouse* will show that the silks of pudding steam have not blurred my critical windows.

My first impression of *In the Glasshouse* was of Helen Tookey's delighted fascination with language:

in the glasshouse we are all listeners
we all make confessions
the air alive as rain whispers *tell us*

'*Tell us*'... Here is a human need, which Tookey hears in the 'urgent language of hunters'. In an assured piece, bordering on prose, her speaker praises shortcuts: 'older ways the body / can read'. Her poems trap intriguing energies: 'Sometimes we are girls, and sometimes horses.' The gateway to this freedom remains language: '*Prairie* is the widest word we know.'

Tookey's own language can be very simple. Her otters are 'thin and / brown and sharp-eyed', yet her words lead gently to the extraordinarily strange: 'She brings you to the ponds, where the people are lying calmly under / the water.' Her poetry remains anchored in a solid world: 'the warm smooth planks of the bridge –'. Even hope is expressed through the body: 'the first slow healings of a broken bone'. Like shattered glass, unfallen for a 'perfect instant', these poems often end in moments of suspension. They can achieve almost magical clarity, like the landscape of a dream: 'this is the place, I have been here before'. They are very easy to read, as if sinking through water to a 'world at last opened / and clear to the touch'. This is a poetry which can reflect our minds' strongest and strangest impressions.

🖎 I would like to single out three pamphlets from which individual poems left particularly sharp impressions. David Wilson's pamphlet *Slope* proved memorable for two contrasting poems. One, 'Summer with Yeats', describes skills needed for successful rock-climbing, in exquisitely light, falling rhythms: 'as / through cold fingers / glittering summer runs'. 'Everest', sad and succinct, describes a mountain ruined by too many climbers: 'a sheet from which the music's fled'. Mark Hinchliffe's *The Raven and the Laughing Head* is quietly eloquent about the dead. 'Pokémon' sets the 'sand spirits' of a game, played by a boy, beside his death, as a soldier, 'on that dusty road [...] north of Laskar Gah'. Elsewhere, there is a warming vision of a library with 'Ted / asking Mrs Gaskell about Emily'. David Attwooll's poems about the Oxford wetland, Otmoor, include wartime memories of music rising from its ditches: 'whole arias from operas sung / by Italian POWs digging there'. In difficult times, it is heartening to read his account of the success of long, local campaigning:

The moor's safe – for now – and free to the people
And the bright cloak of water is home to the birds.

✒ First impressions can be powerful. In 2015, I heard Geraldine Clarkson read one poem. I was captivated by its gusts of energy, from lives often unmentioned in new British poetry. *Declare* turns on twin poles. Its speakers can be intensely practical: 'Bilge goes out with the suds.' They are also haunted by restless spirituality. One title refers to 'Afflatus', the Latin word for divine inspiration. 'We are living like wraiths,' says the speaker. Inner conflict is dramatized in sex: 'my ego an *outré* gent // gaunt with pleasure, opal-strung: he kisses me / slow with garlic tongue'.

Clarkson's puns make a ferocious impression. 'For Our Extinguished Guests' is the story of a nun who leaves her order. (Clarkson's biographical notes mention monastic life.) Her prizewinning poem, 'His Wife in the Corner', compares disappointment in adultery to a teenage failure to buy a jacket. The energy of her enemy's laughter turns to the falling rhythms of the speaker's loss:

and his wife in the corner dressed sharp and rocking violently
her gorgeous green lapels rising and falling with mirth.

If the poems of *Declare* sometimes seem only part of a story, this may be because another pamphlet is forthcoming. Yet the best of Clarkson's work battles with the Church, with lovers, with all the 'rubbish' of the world. *Declare* is shocking, excessive, a brief hurricane of poetry. It is extraordinarily impressive.

SOME CONTRIBUTORS

Zohar Atkins holds a doctorate in Theology from Oxford, where he was a Rhodes Scholar. A fourth-year rabbinical student at The Jewish Theological Seminary, he teaches Torah, dance, and philosophy. His poems have appeared in *Haaretz*, *The Lehrhaus*, *Wave Composition*, *The Oxonian Review*, and elsewhere. **Anthony Barnett**'s collected *Poems & and Translations* were reviewed in *PNR 212*. Other books include critical essays *Antonyms Anew: Barbs & Loves*; and music history: *Listening for Henry Crowder: A Monograph on His Almost Lost Music* and *UnNatural Music: John Lennon & Yoko Ono in Cambridge 1969*. He edits the literary and arts review *Snow lit rev*. **Diana Bridge** lived in China in the 1970s, has a PhD in classical Chinese poetry and is currently working on a collaborative translation of a selection of classical poems. Her *New & Selected* came out earlier this year. **Miles Burrows**'s *Waiting for the Nightingale* will be published in March by Carcanet Press. **Tom Cook**'s poems and criticism have featured in the *New Statesman*, *Spectator*, *TLS* and *Ambit*. He works as a librarian at Oxford University, and is the editor of *Ash* magazine. **Jay Degenhardt** was born in Manchester and studies at the University of Cambridge. His poetry has appeared in *Stirred Press*, *Notes*, *From the Lighthouse*, and on the Young Poets Network. **Mary Durkin** has previously published in *Agenda*, *Acumen*, *The sHop*, and *Magma*. **John Gallas** is a New Zealand poet with eleven volumes out with Carcanet Press and three with Cold Hub (NZ). *The Little Sublime Comedy* will be published by Carcanet in June 2017. He is the 2016 St Magnus Festival poet. **Jane Griffiths** is a Fellow in English at Wadham College, Oxford. Her fifth collection of poems, *Silent in Finisterre*, will be published by Bloodaxe in April. **Ruth Hawthorn** is a lecturer in American Literature at the University of Lincoln. **Katherine Horrex** recently completed a Masters in Creative Writing at the University of Manchester. Her poems have featured in the *Times Literary Supplement*, *Morning Star*, and *Poetry Salzburg Review*. **Marius Kociejowski**'s most recent books are *God's Zoo: Artists, Exiles, Londoners* (Carcanet, 2014), *The Pebble Chance: Feuilletons & Other Prose* (Biblioasis, 2014), and *Zoroaster's Children and Other Travels* (Biblioasis, 2015). Forthcoming titles are *The Notebooks of Arcangelo Riffis* and, a work in progress, *The Serpent Coiled in Naples*. **Jamie Osborn** founded Cambridge Student PEN and was poetry editor at *The Missing Slate*. His translations of Iraqi refugee poems have appeared in *Modern Poetry in Translation*, *Botch*, and elsewhere. **Elise Paschen**'s new book of poetry, *The Nightlife*, will be published in spring 2017. Recent work has appeared in *The New Yorker* and *Poetry*. She teaches in the MFA Writing Program at the School of the Art Institute of Chicago. **Robert Selby** wrote a PhD at Royal Holloway on the life and work of Mick Imlah, and co-edited *Mick Imlah: Selected Prose* (Peter Lang, 2015).

COLOPHON

Editors
Michael Schmidt (General)
Luke Allan (Deputy)

Design
Luke Allan, 2016
Typeset by Little Island Press

Type
PN Review is set in Arnhem, a typeface designed by Fred Smeijers in 1999.

Editorial address
The Editors at the address on the right. Manuscripts cannot be returned unless accompanied by a stamped addressed envelope or international reply coupon.

Subscriptions (6 issues)
individuals: £39/$86
institutions: £49/$105
to: PN Review, Alliance House
30 Cross Street, Manchester
M2 7AQ, UK

Represented by
Compass Independent Publishing
   Services Ltd
Great West House, Great West Road
Brentford TW8 9DF, UK
sales@compass-ips.london

Trade distributors
NBN International
10 Thornbury Road
Plymouth PL6 7PP, UK
orders@nbninternational.com

Copyright
© 2016 Poetry Nation Review
All rights reserved
ISBN 978-1-78410-144-2
ISSN 0144-7076

Supported by